CREATIVE CAREGIVING
and Beyond

DISCLAIMER

Information in this book is provided for general information and educational purposes only and is not offered as legal advice upon which anyone may rely. The law changes. No attorney-client relationship is created by the offering of this information. This firm, Wendy Whiteman Law, does not represent you unless and until it is expressly retained in writing to do so. Legal counsel relating to your individual needs and circumstances is advisable before taking any action that has legal consequences. Consult your tax advisor as well.

ENDORSEMENTS

"*Creative Caregiving and Beyond* is a real-world guide for how to deal with real-world conversations. The aging of America is upon us, and these conversations are inevitably ahead for most of us. This resource will prepare you in advance to know the warning signs and develop a plan for how to allow your aging family members evolve through life's transition with grace, peace, and dignity."

April Anthony
Chief Executive Officer
Encompass Health – Home Health & Hospice

"I was captivated by the real story that Wendy shared as she illustrates the importance of us proactively putting together a plan to take care of our wonderful parents so that they can 'age with dignity,' while we 'keep our sanity.' Wendy shares a specific family's story that makes the emotional underpinnings of family dynamics come alive, if this season of life is not anticipated. *Creative Caregiving and Beyond* provides practical steps around all considerations—caregiving, healthcare, finances, legal documents, etc. A must-read for everyone, but especially those who have parents or family nearing their elder years."

Diane Paddison
Founder and Executive Director of 4word (www.4wordwomen.org).
Author of Work, Love, Pray and Be Refreshed
Former Global Executive Team—Fortune 500 and Fortune 1000 companies (COO, Trammell Crow Company and ProLogis; President, Corporate Services, Client)

"The story is engaging and talks of meaningful struggles (and how to get out of them) in a way that is straightforward and easy to follow!"

C. Sue Sullins
Film Documentarian

"Wendy Whiteman has written a thoughtful book on caring for aging parents. With the dramatic growth of baby boomers retiring, this is an extremely helpful guide. It offers both clarity and dignity to elder care."

Dr. Mac Pier
Founder, Movement.org

"This is a realistic family, with realistic issues, that provides readers with a straightforward approach to elderly care. The book takes a holistic approach while covering all of the dynamics involved when taking care of elderly parents."

Kathryn Waldrep
Founding Partner Vernon & Waldrep OB-Gyn Assoc.
OBGYN Board-Certified
D Magazine, Voted as " Best Doctors in Dallas"
Southern Methodist University "Profile in Leadership Award"
2015 Christian Union's "Texas Christian of the Year"

"This story could not be more timely given the rate of our nation's aging population; there are forty-six million who are sixty-five years and older living in the US. Demographers project this number will exceed ninety million by 2050. This book provides essential information that will help caregivers become more effective in addressing this enormous challenge. I highly recommend this book for those who will be faced with this immense responsibility."

Henry W. Foster, Jr., MD, FACOG
Professor Emeritus, former
Vice President for Medical Services & Dean
School of Medicine - Meharry Medical College
Clinical Professor, Obstetrics and Gynecology - Vanderbilt University
Former (Nominee) United States Surgeon General

Helping Mom and Dad

WENDY WILLIAMS WHITEMAN

EQUIP PRESS

Colorado Springs

Copyright © 2020 Wendy Williams Whiteman

All rights reserved. No part of this publication may be reproduced, distributed, or transmitted in any form or by any means, without prior written permission.

Published by Equip Press, Colorado Springs, CO

Contemporary English Version (CEV) Copyright © 1995 by American Bible Society

The Holy Bible, English Standard Version. The Holy Bible, English Standard Version. ESV® Text Edition: 2016. Copyright © 2001 by Crossway Bibles, a publishing ministry of Good News Publishers.

Scripture quotations marked (ESV) are taken from The ESV® Bible (The Holy Bible, English Standard Version®) copyright © 2001 by Crossway, a publishing ministry of Good News Publishers. ESV® Text Edition: 2011. The ESV® text has been reproduced in cooperation with and by permission of Good News Publishers.

Unauthorized reproduction of this publication is prohibited. Used by permission. All rights reserved.

Scripture quotations marked (KJV) are taken from the King James Bible. Accessed on Bible Gateway at www.BibleGateway.com.

Scripture quotations marked (NASB) are taken from the New American Standard Bible® (NASB), copyright © 1960, 1962, 1963, 1968, 1971, 1972, 1973, 1975, 1977, 1995 by The Lockman Foundation, www.Lockman.org. Used by permission.

Scripture quotations marked (NIV) are taken from the Holy Bible, New International Version. Copyright © 1973, 1978, 1984, 2011 by Biblica, Inc.® Used by permission. All rights reserved worldwide.

Scripture quotations marked (NKJV) are taken from the New King James Version®. Copyright © 1982 by Thomas Nelson, Inc. Used by permission. All rights reserved.

Scripture quotations marked (NLT) are taken from the Holy Bible, New Living Translation, copyright © 1996, 2004, 2015 by Tyndale House Foundation. Used by permission of Tyndale House Publishers, Inc., Carol Stream, Illinois 60188. All rights reserved.

Scripture quotations marked (NRSV) are taken from the New Revised Standard Version Bible, copyright © 1989 the Division of Christian Education of the National Council of the Churches of Christ in the United States of America. Used by permission. All rights reserved.

First Edition: 2020
Creative Caregiving and Beyond / Wendy Williams Whiteman
Paperback ISBN: 978-1-951304-15-7
eBook ISBN: 978-1-951304-16-4

DEDICATION

I dedicate this book to my mother, Arthulena Williams. My mother, who was known as Ms. A in many circles, overcame tremendous odds as a sharecropper's daughter to become the first in her family to receive college and graduate degrees. As a teacher of talented and gifted students for many years, she dedicated her life to helping scores of students develop their God-given talents and gifts, inspiring them to dream beyond their visible potential. She inspired me to be the person that I am today, and to write this book. In our loved ones' golden seasons, though they may not be the same people they were in their prime, we must remember that they have made valuable contributions to our lives, as well as the lives of many others. Keeping these things in perspective allows us to properly appreciate their lives and treat them in the manner they deserve to be treated as children of God.

I can do all things through Christ which strengtheneth me.
(PHIL. 4:13 KJV)

CONTENTS

Dedication	11
Acknowledgment	15
The Elder Family Tree	17
The Elder Family	19
Introduction	21

Having the Conversation — 23
- Email from George to Elizabeth, Susie, and Trevor — 23
- Thanksgiving Day — 24
- What Happens Next? — 26
- Lessons Learned — 27
- Reflective Questions — 30

Doing It Right the First Time — 31
- Regrouping — 31
- The List — 32
- Lessons Learned — 35
- Reflective Questions — 36

Getting Mom and Dad Organized — 37
- What to Organize — 41
- The Siblings — 42
- Lessons Learned — 42
- Reflective Questions — 44

Who's in Charge? — 45
- Assigning Responsibility — 45
- The Elder Story Continues — 48
- Elizabeth — 48
- George — 50
- Trevor — 52
- Susie — 52
- Walter — 53
- At the Hospital — 54
- Lessons Learned — 55
- Reflective Questions — 58

Relationship Dynamics — 59
- Family Dynamics — 60
- Walter Comes Home — 61
- Friends — 64
- The Caregiver Arrives — 64
- Assisted-Living Community — 66
- Walter Fades — 67
- Issues You May Face — 68
- Lessons Learned — 70
- Reflective Questions — 71

Keeping Your Sanity and Their Dignity — 73
- The Toll of Caregiving — 73
- Maintaining Your Sanity — 74
- Caregiver Burnout — 74
- Avoid Caregiver Burnout — 76
- Choose Empowerment — 76
- Take Care of Yourself — 77
- Keeping Their Dignity — 79
- What Does This Mean for Your Sanity and Their Dignity? — 81
- What's Next — 82
- Reflective Questions — 82

Help to the Rescue! — 85
- Be Willing to Ask for Help — 85
- Can Your Employer Help? — 87
- Engage Others in the Responsibilities — 87
- Vetting, Selecting, and Managing Caregivers — 88
- Technology Can Help! — 89
- Integration — 89
- Reflective Questions — 90

Estate Planning Essentials — 91
- Protecting Yourself — 91
- Estate Planning Documents — 93
- Who Makes Critical Decisions? — 95
- Reflective Questions — 96

You Can Do This! — 97

ACKNOWLEDGMENT

I would like to acknowledge the love and support of my husband, Gregg, who is the most patient man I know. His steadfast belief in me is beyond expression, and I thank you.

I also thank my son, Cash, who inspires me every day and has made it such a joy for me to be a mom; my brother, Del, who has teamed with me in the support of my mother; my mother's caregivers, especially Erika, Danielle, and Theresa, who the Lord truly sent to help us! Thanks to my dream team staff, Kelli and Patty; Brenda, Felecia, and Aldonna at KSG, who kept my office running flawlessly as I navigated this process. Also, thank you to my dear friends, Kim and Sue, who have been spiritual rocks for me. To many other family and friends who have encouraged and prayed for me along the way—I thank you!

Special Thanks:

Cover Design by Kelli Fore
Cover Artwork by Cash Whiteman (2006)

THE ELDER FAMILY TREE

The Elder Family Tree

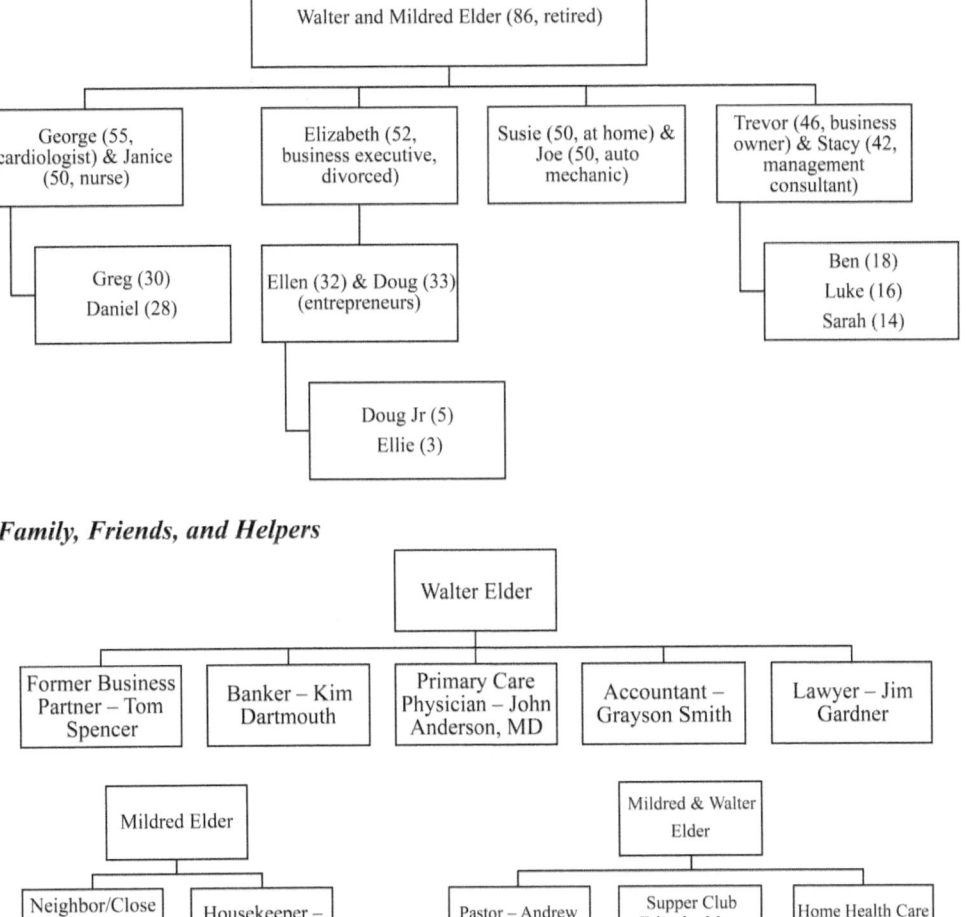

Family, Friends, and Helpers

THE ELDER FAMILY

This is the story of the Elder family, and the following is a synopsis, of the storyline we will follow throughout this book.
- Mildred and Walter Elder are the patriarchs. They've been married for sixty years, are quite independent, and what some would describe as stubborn. Mildred and Walter are both eighty-six and have been healthy throughout their lives. They have four grown children. Mildred was a teacher at the local high school for many years, and Walter was a colonel in the air force. He retired from military service and then created a successful business with a college friend, Tom Spencer. Mildred and Walter have lived in the same house for fifty years.
- George, Mildred and Walter's son, is a fifty-five-year-old cardiologist and is married to Janice, who is a nurse. They live in the same city as Mildred and Walter.
    o They have two sons: Greg, who is thirty, and Daniel, twenty-eight. Both live in the same city as Mildred and Walter.
- Elizabeth, Mildred and Walter's daughter, is fifty-two, divorced, and lives three states away from Mildred and Walter. Elizabeth is a business executive in a Fortune 100 company. She has a daughter, Ellen, who is thirty-two.
    o Ellen is married to Doug, and they have two children: Doug Jr., five, and Ellie, three. Ellen and Doug are entrepreneurs who own a home-based business. They live in a small town about fifty miles away from Mildred and Walter.
- Susie, Mildred and Walter's daughter, is fifty and does not work. Her husband, Joe, is an auto mechanic who works seven days

a week. They do not have kids. She and her husband live in a suburb of the city where Mildred and Walter live. Susie has never been very close to the rest of the family and often borrows money from her parents to make ends meet. Several years ago, George, the eldest brother, found out about the many loans Susie got from their parents that she never paid back.

- Trevor, Mildred and Walter's son, is forty-six, owns a small printing business, and is married to Stacy, who is a busy management consultant, traveling about 20 percent of the time. Trevor borrowed money from Mildred and Walter to start his printing business, setting the loan up on a ten-year payback. Most of the time, Trevor pays the interest-free loan on time. They live in a town about fifty miles away from Mildred and Walter. They have three kids.
  - Ben is eighteen
  - Luke is sixteen
  - Sarah is fourteen

Over the past year, George and Janice have noticed that Walter seems more forgetful and is not always processing information well. He was in the military for a long time and has always been sharp-minded, a bit of a commander type. He still does things like trying to climb up a ladder to clean the gutters on his house, and they are concerned that the house is getting to be too much for him. Mildred has always been very sweet and does whatever Walter tells her to do. She doesn't know anything about their finances, mortgages, assets, or investments.

INTRODUCTION

As we all know, life has many seasons, and that's okay. We must make the necessary adaptations to them; however, this may prove difficult, especially for the elderly. Life is precious at every stage, so it becomes our call to assist the elderly in adapting to their greatest season. In this book, I promise to explain, inform, and equip you with the skills to help yourself and anyone around you who is facing these changes.

I didn't feel the need to write this book until I began the journey as a caregiver for my mom. I've counseled and represented thousands of families going through the process of helping their parents as they age. I've worked with families at different stages, from simply getting Mom and Dad organized and decluttered after decades of accumulation to becoming a quasi-detective in their parents' lives. Family members often needed to find out what assets their parents owned and how they could preserve those assets from diminishing during a catastrophic illness.

No matter the stage, several dynamics come into play. We will examine these stages or themes and offer some helpful solutions.

- Having the Conversation
- Doing It Right the First Time
- Getting Mom and Dad Organized
- Who's in Charge?
- Relationship Dynamics
- Keeping Your Sanity and Their Dignity
- Help to the Rescue!
- Estate Planning Essentials

To protect the confidentiality of clients and to make this book more usable, I'm using a storyline about a typical family dealing with elder family members. Then, based on the story, I provide lessons learned and best practices. The storyline is based on my thirty-plus years of legal practice.

My sincere hope is that this book will guide you along the path of caring for and respecting elder parents, other relatives, and friends, and dealing with the issues that come with the changes in their lives and the lives of their loved ones.

HAVING THE CONVERSATION

> The right word at the right time is like precious gold set in silver.
>
> — **PROVERBS 25:11 CEV**

Based on their observations described in the synopsis, George and Janice decide it's time to involve the other siblings in their growing concerns. George sends an email out to everyone about three weeks before Thanksgiving because all the siblings will be together at Walter and Mildred's home on Thanksgiving Day.

Email from George to Elizabeth, Susie, and Trevor

Hello, Everyone,

I trust this email finds everyone in good spirits. I'll get right to the point. Janice and I have been spending a little more time with Mom and Dad lately, and we are concerned about them trying to manage that big house by themselves. We've noticed Dad being forgetful about things, and that is out of character for him. Mom said that once while she was taking a nap, he drove the car to the grocery store to pick up a few things and couldn't remember how to get home. She thought it was funny, but I'm not sure she realizes that may indicate a problem. Daniel and Greg went over to visit them last week, and Daniel said Mom kept getting their names mixed up.

So we feel like we should talk to them over the holidays and let them know that we are concerned. There are some posh facilities they could go to where they would be comfortable, or there are home healthcare options. My other concern is how these memory lapses may be affecting their finances and other decisions.

Please email me back or call me in the evening with your thoughts.

Regards, George

Response to All from Elizabeth
"Thanks, George. Why don't you handle this? You are close to them, and I just don't have a lot of time to devote to any of it, especially with my travel schedule."

Response to All from Susie
"George, I think you are overreacting. Old people forget stuff. I think they are fine where they are."

Response to All from Trevor
"I see what you are saying, George. Why don't we speak to them after dinner on Thanksgiving, when we are all around and relaxed?"

Thanksgiving Day

After Thanksgiving dinner, in the early afternoon, George calls his siblings, Elizabeth, Susie, and Trevor into the living room with their mom and dad. The spouses, kids, and grandkids go to the movies to give them some privacy for the conversation.

George says, "Mom, Dad, we really appreciate all you have done for us through the years. You've worked hard all your life, and we're concerned that maybe this house is too big for you guys."

Walter stands up, obviously annoyed and says, "I don't need to hear this! I am just fine. George, I can't believe you are trying to shove me out of my own house!"

Mildred says, "Well, speak for yourself, Walter, I think George is just trying to help."

"Well, he isn't!" says Walter as he storms out of the room. Mildred dutifully follows her husband out of the room.

Susie says sarcastically, "Great job, George. I knew this would happen."

George looks down his nose at Susie and says, "Well, maybe you are afraid of losing the gravy train."

Elizabeth and Trevor look at each other as if to ask, "What is George talking about?"

Susie starts to cry and yells, "You just don't understand!" and leaves the room.

George apologizes to Elizabeth and Trevor for mishandling the conversation with their parents and suggests that they spend a little time figuring out their next strategy. George dismisses their questions about Susie's reaction.

Elizabeth points out that their dad probably felt like the kids were ganging up on him. As a retired air force colonel, he's used to being in charge of things and may have a lot of pride around these issues, even if he knows he's not in tip-top mental capacity anymore.

Trevor points out that their mom might be helpful in talking to him because she seems more open to making a change. While she has always done whatever he told her to do, he is very protective of her and will listen to what she has to say about her own needs.

Elizabeth finally says, "Why don't you let me talk to Mom and see how she is feeling about possibly going to an upscale retirement community? If we show them where they could go, they might be more willing to accept it."

Trevor wonders out loud if they should figure out how their parents are doing financially and how they would fund the upscale retirement community. George says he knows their banker, Kim Dartmouth. While the banker cannot give them specific information about their parents' finances, they can at least give the banker a heads-up that the siblings are concerned about their dad's memory and decision-making.

When Mildred returns to the room, Elizabeth suggests they take a walk and learns that Mildred is feeling a little overwhelmed with the house and cooking for her husband every day. She knows nothing of their finances and wonders if she should know more in case something happens to him. She confides that she hasn't told him any of this because he seems grumpier in his old age. Elizabeth is a bright businesswoman and gets permission from her mom to do a little investigation of their finances. Mildred seems relieved and discusses with Elizabeth how to bring up the subject to Walter to let him know how she's feeling. Elizabeth changes her flights so she can stay over a few extra days.

Susie has disappeared, driving off after leaving the family meeting.

When Walter comes back in the room, George apologizes and says he was insensitive in the way he handled things. Walter accepts the apology and changes the subject.

What Happens Next?

The day after Thanksgiving when everyone has gone home except for Elizabeth, she does a little investigation. In looking through her parents' bank statements, insurance policies, and other documentation, she discovers some rather large withdrawals from their home account that were paid to an individual.

Elizabeth asks her mom, "Who is Mary Stotzer?"

Mildred explains that she is someone from their supper club who has fallen on hard times. "I guess Dad felt sorry for her because she's been our friend for over thirty years," she said. When Elizabeth tells her mom the amount, Mildred asks, "Can we afford that?"

Elizabeth also discovers some large stock sales but can't track where the money went. She suggests they get Walter's buy-in on getting financial help or allowing Elizabeth to help them keep track of things. Mildred, for the first time in her life, realizes she can't blindly let Walter handle everything.

Elizabeth calls Trevor and suggests that he refinance his business loan with a bank or other lender because their parents can't afford to carry the note. Trevor reluctantly agrees. He doesn't say anything but feels like Elizabeth is taking over everything. He calls George to complain.

Since George is in the doghouse with his dad, Elizabeth decides to call Tom Spencer, her dad's longtime friend and former business partner, to see if he can help. This is a man whom Walter trusts, so perhaps Walter will agree to accept help.

Ultimately, Walter's former business partner gets him to agree to get some help managing his finances and to get checked regarding his memory loss and confusion. Tom convinces him it can't hurt anything, and he might even prove to his smarty-pants son that he got it wrong.

Lessons Learned

The Elder family scenario represents some key points about "having the conversation." Some things didn't work out so well, but the siblings figured out how to re-strategize by leveraging the strongest relationship connection between Mildred and Elizabeth. Here are the key learning points we can pull from the story.

Plan Something Other Than an Ambush

As you can see from the story, the father felt ambushed, even though he needed help desperately. Gathering the siblings to have a talk with their parents obviously backfired. A better strategy emerged, but people storming out of the room could have been avoided. If one or two of the children had approached their father and mother without the whole clan present, the outcome might have been very different.

When someone feels attacked, it's human nature to demonstrate fight-or-flight behavior, which Walter did by getting mad and running out of the room. Susie showed flight, as she felt attacked by what George said and left the house. Even though George and the siblings were well-intentioned, the first strategy didn't work.

The good news is that if something like this does happen, you can always step back and re-strategize. This is where watching for opportunities can come into play.

Watch for Opportunities

The siblings noticed that their mother might be more open to making a change. Assigning Elizabeth to talk one-on-one with her mother opened a door to convincing the parents to accept that they needed help. Their mom's willingness about possibly moving out of the house would open that conversation with her dad at some point. Mildred's reaction to the large amount of money her husband gave to a friend was an opportunity for Elizabeth to figure out how to get her dad to seek help with his financial decisions.

Use Effective Communication That Parents Will Accept

Elizabeth knew her father needed to hear about getting help from someone he respected. As a take-charge man, she knew it would be difficult to hear the message from one of the children, especially after the way the family meeting had played out.

The siblings made a wise decision to put George in the background and leverage Elizabeth's relationship with their mother. Elizabeth's approach was one of discovery. She discovered some things that her mom might even be hesitant to share with her husband.

Elizabeth's manner of finding out her mom's feelings about the situation opened the door. Ultimately, Mildred realized that she needed to get more involved in the financial decisions or at least be aware of what Walter was doing with their money.

Allow Elder Family Members to Express How They Feel About a Change

While a family meeting is a good way to have a conversation with elder loved ones about making a change, sometimes it will come across wrong. In this case, asking the parents how they felt about managing the big house in a casual conversation might have allowed Mildred to express her struggles with managing the house and her duties. Every scenario in a family will be a little different. You must figure out the best way to discuss changes with elder loved ones that make the most sense for your family's situation.

In the scenario, Walter felt like something was being pushed on him. No one asked his opinion about continuing the upkeep of the family home, so he resisted even more out of pride. If Walter was approached differently, based on his personality type and relationship history with the family, he might have reacted to George's suggestions differently. Giving him more autonomy and control of his situation would allow him to be more open-minded about what his children were trying to communicate to him.

Keep Their Dignity

Your parents likely supported and raised you, your whole life. Even if they faltered along the way and you have unresolved issues with them, they still want to feel they have some authority and control over their lives. In some cases, they are not as mobile as they used to be, or their brain function is not as keen due to the aging process. Talking down to or verbalizing your frustration only creates more stress for them.

Consider how you might feel if you could no longer remember simple things or could not move around as fast as you used to. It can be frustrating. Your elder loved ones don't need to be reminded of their limitations. Truly, some will become belligerent due to their mental state. You might have to let some of it go and learn to ignore it, knowing this can be a normal part of aging.

Stay as upbeat as you can. Your attitude can be an inspiration to your elder loved one. An article at psychologytoday.com states, "A new study by researchers in Ireland reports that having a positive attitude about aging may help prevent older adults from becoming frail, which, in turn, appears to keep their minds sharp. On the flip side, the researchers confirmed that having negative attitudes about the aging effect both physical and cognitive health in later years. The researchers concluded, 'Negative perceptions of aging may modify the association between frailty and frontal cognitive domains in older adults.'"[1]

Your attitude toward your elder loved one should support lifting them up rather than tearing them down, even though you are dealing with your own frustrations. This is a journey best traveled in a partnership as positive as possible.

---

1 https://www.psychologytoday.com/us/blog/the-athletes-way/201601/positive-attitudes-about-aging-may-be-fountain-youth

While having the conversation is an important first step to managing the situation with your elder loved ones, thoroughly assessing the situation is equally important. Getting your elder loved ones organized can include their household belongings, finances, and medical and legal documentation.

REFLECTIVE QUESTIONS

- Have you thought about having a conversation with your elderly parents about their situation?
- Who should be present?
- What resistance or issues do you anticipate?
- How would you deal with the issues?

DOING IT RIGHT THE FIRST TIME

> If you don't have time to do it right,
> when will you have time to do it over?
>
> — JOHN WOODEN

After the Thanksgiving episode, George, Elizabeth, and Trevor realized that some things needed to change. They emailed and spoke to each other over the phone in the weeks between Thanksgiving and Christmas. Susie was invited to all these calls but did not engage with the other siblings. Each of the siblings also discussed the situation with their spouses and confidants.

As they continue to communicate with their parents, it's clear they need to "do it right the first time" to avoid another blowup.

Regrouping

Elizabeth realizes she will need to take a bigger role than anticipated. She returns to her hectic position as a business executive and realizes that until they get Mom and Dad settled, she may need to make some changes. She has coffee with her business mentor to get some ideas.

Her mentor suggests that she get her daughter Ellen to help. Ellen and her husband, Doug Jr., have a home-based business and live fifty miles from Mildred and Walter. Most of their work is done online, so spending more time with Mildred and Walter is feasible. In addition, Elizabeth and her mentor agree that she should consider doing more work remotely or delegating some of her duties at work. Elizabeth considers other options that will make her schedule more flexible.

George and Janice know they need to mend the fence with Dad, so George starts by taking his dad out to lunch and apologizing for the Thanksgiving episode. George also knows that Susie and her husband are probably the only ones who will join Mom and Dad for Christmas dinner, and all the other siblings will go to their in-laws.' Elizabeth typically takes a trip around Christmas to escape her hectic corporate life. George does not want Susie to take advantage of the fact that Dad is mad at him.

At lunch, George apologizes and says he just "had it wrong." George doesn't really believe that, but he's willing to swallow his pride for the sake of his relationship with his dad. George and Janice also talk to their sons, Daniel and Greg, who can help locally with some tasks. Neither of them is married at this point, and they both live and work in the same town as their grandparents.

Trevor works on getting his business loan refinanced. On some level, he knows that the terms of the loan were probably unfair to the other siblings. Relationships are important to him, and he doesn't want to create bad blood with his siblings.

Trevor's wife Stacy, who is a management consultant, focuses on getting more local clients to free up some time from her travel schedule. This will give Trevor the opportunity to spend more time helping his parents.

Susie does not engage in any of this. Inside, she is slightly panicked because she realizes that things will probably change drastically in the next few months.

One thing most of the children realize is that they need to step back and create an intentional plan, deciding how much help their parents need and who will take care of what.

The List

Elizabeth is the most organized of the group and has the closest relationship with her mom and dad, so she comes up with a list of items to determine how they need to help their parents. Although she told the group she would make a list, she made it clear that they could not come across like they are telling their parents what to do, especially Dad. Here's what she came up with:

- Getting Organized
    - Legal documents - Estate, will, power of attorney
    - Financial accounts and documents
    - House/garage/storage unit
    - Medications/doctors
    - Contact information
- Decisions to Make
    - Living arrangements - Keep the house or move
    - Legal structures - Living trusts, power of attorney (POA)
    - Financial management
    - Health management
    - Preburial plans (let them bring it up, do not mention)
    - Who's in charge of what
- How to Keep the Peace
    - Sensitive to Dad's need to be in charge
    - Siblings work as a team, all for the same result
    - Understanding Susie's situation
    - Get the kids (grandkids) to be involved
- Research
    - Living facilities/home health care
    - Tax implications
    - Good legal counsel
    - Medicaid/Medicare/payment for helpers if one of them gets sick

Elizabeth shares the list with her siblings, and they have nothing to add to it. The next big task is to figure out who is in charge of what. Since the holidays are coming up, everyone decides they can leave much of this until after the first of the year. Elizabeth cancels her annual ski trip and goes home for Christmas.

In light of the situation, George and Janice decide not to go to Janice's family gathering. Instead, they ask if they can host Christmas dinner. Mildred is thrilled. Though she has been the great family entertainer for years, she is having trouble standing for long periods of time. Susie is not thrilled with this arrangement.

At Christmas, George, Janice, and Elizabeth are glad not to talk about all that is going on with their parents because moving into this new season of helping them is daunting. Susie is happy the situation isn't being discussed, but for different reasons.

At the dinner table, Walter tells a story about something that happened a few days ago. He lost his screwdriver in the garage and a neighbor came over to help him find it. Then in the middle of the story, he gets it confused with another story about when he and the neighbor were looking for the bicycle pump in the garage. Everyone at the table gets quiet. Elizabeth and George look at each other with concern because this type of forgetfulness is uncharacteristic of their father. He seems more confused than they have ever seen him. Susie just keeps looking at her plate, not connecting with her siblings. Her husband Joe follows her lead on being silent.

Mildred laughs and says, "Oh, Walter, you get confused about these little things these days."

Walter fires back, "You don't have such a good memory either!"

Again, George and Elizabeth look at each other because the outburst at their mother is out of character.

Mildred apologizes and attempts to smooth over the situation, and then changes the subject to the delicious meal they have just enjoyed. She thanks Janice and George for working so hard on the meal and mentions that they have saved her a lot of back pain! Susie thanks them too and says, "It's the best Christmas meal ever, even if you didn't make Mom's famous rolls."

After dinner, Elizabeth and George talk out of earshot of their parents and resolve to follow up with each other about their dad's behavior. The situation makes both of them think they need to do more investigation and perhaps step up their plan for helping their parents.

Elizabeth goes back home with her parents that evening since she is staying there until New Year's Day. She had planned to put off thinking about the whole thing until after the first of the year, but now she realizes she had better step it up a bit. While she's there, Elizabeth figures maybe she can help them get organized, which will help her figure out what she and her siblings need to do.

Lessons Learned

Planning Ahead

Thinking ahead of time, as Elizabeth did when she made the list, will help ensure that things are done right the first time. Her parents may not have shown her that they need help organizing their medications and medical contacts, for example, but thinking about it ahead of time could avoid a serious situation in an emergency.

Even though Elizabeth wanted to put off planning and working with her parents through the situation, she and George realized they needed to take action right away.

In dealing with your elders, taking action sooner rather than later is always a good idea.

Pay Attention

Observation of the changes in elder loved ones' behavior can be a telling sign of the onslaught of dementia. Dad was telling a story about something that happened recently and got confused in the middle of it. Also, his reaction to his wife was out of character and angry, which is another sign.

What do you notice about your elder loved ones? Subtle behavior changes can be telling signs of changing mental capacity. It's key not to make assumptions about their behavior just because they are old. [2]

Maintaining Their Dignity

The children, especially George, learned a valuable lesson at Thanksgiving. Doing it right the first time will always include considering

---

2   My interview with Delwin Williams, MD, Psychiatrist at John Peter Smith Hospital, Ft. Worth, Texas, July 2019.

how elder loved ones feel. Those who have been in charge of their lives for so many years and accomplished so much will likely find it hard to let their children manage things. Feeling like you don't have control of your memory, as Walter might feel, is humbling and scary.

Regarding burial plans, it's good to mention it carefully. Preplanning while a person is healthy ensures that there's adequate time to walk through all their wishes, including what they want at their services, such as songs and flowers.

Remember, the endgame is to get elder loved ones to cooperate and not feel bad about what may not be in place. Approach them with tact so they are willing to explore getting organized with their long-term care and estate plan.

REFLECTIVE QUESTIONS

- Have you noticed your elder loved ones getting confused or forgetting something that happened recently?
- What do you need to know about your parents' situation that you don't know now?
- What do you need to do to maintain your parents' dignity in these early planning stages?

GETTING MOM AND DAD ORGANIZED

The next day, Elizabeth makes breakfast for her parents, and then they retire to the sunroom to enjoy more coffee. Dad doesn't stay long. He likes to keep moving, so he excuses himself.

Elizabeth asks her mom what she wants to do today, and her mom says, "You know, maybe you can help me clean out that extra bedroom upstairs. There's just so much junk in there."

Elizabeth, who loves to organize things, agrees it's a terrific idea. When they get up to the room, she is a bit surprised to find it difficult to even walk through the room. She asks her mom about it.

"Oh, this is kinda like the junk drawer I always had in the kitchen. If I can't figure out where to put something, I just put it in here."

Elizabeth asks, "Do you mind if I help you organize it?"

"Of course not," Mom replies.

"Your dad will probably not let you help with the mess in the garage, but that's his problem!"

They both laugh because Walter has always been stubborn about people interfering with his garage.

Elizabeth finds everything from old bank statements to old clothes and items that look like they need to be given away. Her mom explains that she would give stuff away, but she keeps thinking she might need it for something. She says, "You know, I remember when you and Susie were home, you used to fight over which one of you would get to wear the prized prom dress. And when you were younger, you always would fuss about who got to play with the Raggedy Ann dolls. I can't bear to part with them."

Elizabeth decides that it might take some convincing to get her mom to let go of things, so for the moment, she stores the possible giveaways in the corner. She gets her mom to help her put all the bank statements in one pile. She also finds a bunch of receipts lying around.

Mom says, "Your dad always kept receipts for everything for tax write-offs. I don't know which ones he still needs, so I keep all of them."

They stack all the receipts in a pile.

Elizabeth is alarmed to find a handwritten will in a drawer. She asks her mother about it.

Mildred replies, "One of Walter's friends convinced him that he could write his own will and didn't have to have a notary sign it, as long as he wrote the whole will in longhand."

Elizabeth asks her mom where they keep their legal documents like wills and real estate documents.

"Walter keeps most of the stuff in a plastic bag in the freezer in the garage so they don't get stolen or lost in a fire."

Elizabeth has not heard that one before, but it seems reasonable that they wouldn't be lost in a fire, and she and her siblings would have easy access if they need them.

This goes on most of the day. As the day progresses, Elizabeth convinces her mom that they could shred or throw away some of the documents. Elizabeth asks if she can confirm that with Walter and their accountant, and Mom thinks that is a good idea.

Elizabeth notices some other things going on with her parents and realizes that she should help them organize those as well. Her mom needs to refill a prescription, but Elizabeth can't find it anywhere and has to help her mom remember where the doctor's and pharmacy's phone numbers are.

Elizabeth asks, "Hey, Mom, would it help if I got all that medical information organized for you?"

"Well," Mildred says with a smile, "it looks like I could use some organization."

"Mom, do you have a list of all of the medications you and Dad are currently taking?"

"Oh, no, I'm not very good about that. I just take what the doctor recommends. We can look around for prescriptions and figure it out."

Elizabeth is concerned with Mildred's lax attitude about it, so she decides to take more action.

"Mom," she asks, "could we contact your doctor and get the office to help us get these medications organized? They will not give information directly to me, but they will give it to you. And what about Dad? Can you get him to allow me to speak to his doctor?"

"Well, I don't know if he will agree, but I'm glad to ask him. You know he is very proud. He doesn't like people meddling in his business."

Elizabeth says, "Let's at least call your doctor's office tomorrow and see if they can help us out."

"Okay, honey, that sounds like a good idea."

Elizabeth offers to order in food because she doesn't feel like cooking, and she is concerned about her mom being too tired after a long day of organizing. She figures out what they would like, picks it up, and brings it home. They eat, just making small talk.

Later that evening, Elizabeth and her parents are relaxing by the fire after dinner. Elizabeth thinks this relaxed atmosphere is a good time to approach her dad about getting organized.

"Dad, how was your day?" she asks.

"Oh, pretty good. I went over and had lunch with Tom Spencer at the golf club. We talked about memories of our business. Funny how I can remember details about that but forget where I put the screwdriver," he answers with a smile. "Then I went and puttered around in my garage."

"That sounds great, Dad. Mom and I worked on organizing the extra bedroom upstairs. We found some bank statements, papers, and receipts that you probably don't need anymore. Can we throw some of that stuff out?"

"Well, I don't know. You know I have to keep records from that business Tom and I had."

"Dad, some of the stuff we found is fifteen years old. Can I double-check with your accountant to make sure it's okay to get rid of some of it?"

"Elizabeth, you are a smart businesswoman. I trust you to talk to my accountant. That would probably help your mom and me."

"Thanks, Dad. I wonder if you have other things I can help you and Mom organize? I know your garage and the storage unit are full of things that you might not need anymore. Maybe Daniel and Greg could help you move out what you don't need."

Elizabeth knows she needs to tread softly, yet it is time to get her parents more organized just in case something happens to one of them.

"Well, I guess that wouldn't hurt," Walter answers. "I haven't been over to the storage unit in a while. I might not even need it, so it would be good to get rid of it. One less thing to think about."

Mildred says, "You know, Walter, today I was looking for my prescription so I could refill it, and I realized I'm pretty disorganized with that information. Elizabeth has offered to help us organize the prescriptions and doctor information. She would need for you to go with her to your doctor to get some of the information. What do you think?"

"Well, it sure feels like you are trying to take over my life, Elizabeth," said Walter, looking down his nose over the top of his glasses at Elizabeth.

"I can appreciate that, Dad. I know you don't want others telling you what to do. I just want to make sure that everything is organized for you guys so you don't have to worry about it."

"Well, I'm not worried. I'm healthy as a horse," Walter declares.

Elizabeth decides she probably needs to drop the subject for now. At least she can get her mom's information organized and probably do a little digging to find out about her dad's doctors and prescriptions.

Walter says, "Well, it's time for my reading time. I'll be in my study."

After Walter leaves the room, Mildred says, "Well, at least I can go into the medicine cabinet and let you know what prescriptions he is taking."

Elizabeth asks her mom if she can take pictures of the labels with her cell phone. Mildred laughs and says, "Well, I can sure try. I've gotten pretty good with that thing."

Elizabeth knows that each bottle will at least have the doctor's name, pharmacy information, prescription, and dosage. That is a step in the right direction.

Elizabeth makes calls to Daniel and Greg, asking them to help their grandfather. They eagerly agree, as they are both concerned about his failing memory.

Elizabeth makes a list of what she noticed and what she needed to organize. She wants to share it with her siblings so that everyone will know what is going on. Her next task is to get the siblings on board with everyone's role. Here's what she put on the list.

What to Organize

- Old Documents
    - Accountant - What to get rid of
- Bank
    - Contact banker
    - Organize statements
- Legal
    - Handwritten will
    - Meet with lawyer
    - Get legal documents in order, including a medical power of attorney
    - Check out documents in the freezer in the garage
- House/garage/storage unit
    - Greg and Daniel help clean out garage and storage unit
    - Yard work - Someone has been mowing it, but shrubs and other landscaping are in bad shape
    - House upkeep - Parts of the house have not been cleaned in a while
    - Repairs - Kitchen sink leaking, gutter broken, sidewalk bricks crumbling
- Medical
    - Organize prescriptions, doctor, and pharmacy information
    - Understand what prescriptions are for and possible side effects
    - Emergency medical plan

The Siblings

Elizabeth calls Susie to explain what she found.

Susie replies, "Well, I already knew she had a junk room. It's her business if she just wants to throw stuff in there."

Elizabeth decides not to try convincing Susie otherwise and replied that she just wanted to keep Susie in the loop. They abruptly end the phone call.

Elizabeth then calls George and Trevor to let them know what is going on and that she will need their help getting their parents organized and keeping things in order. She shares that she wanted to make sure their legal and financial documents were in order and also wanted to make sure they had the right documents in place in case something happened to one of their parents.

Elizabeth ends her day creating a spreadsheet of the medical information she was able to get from prescription bottles and her mother's memory. She emails the document to George for safekeeping and so he can respond to any concerns about the drugs they were taking. It would make sense for George to discuss his dad's medical conditions with his doctor, but right now, George was still in the doghouse from the Thanksgiving debacle.

Lessons Learned

Observe the Landscape

Nothing is more telling than doing a little digging into how elders live. Elizabeth didn't know about the extra bedroom that looked like a hoarder lived there. She discovers that legal documents are not all in the same place and that a holographic (handwritten) will is stuffed in a drawer. She also finds old and unnecessary documents, which can create more for her parents to manage. Even something as simple as her mom's inability to find her prescription and the phone numbers for the doctor and the pharmacy is a red flag, confirming the need to help her parents get organized. She notices some repairs her dad would typically take care of that either he hadn't noticed or just let go. Because Elizabeth had thought about what *could be* ahead of time by making the list, she piqued her sensitivity to what to look for at her parents' home.

Ask Questions

Elizabeth is always keen to ask for her parents' input. She doesn't go in there and tell them they should throw away this and that. She asks questions and, in doing so, allows them to feel like they are in control. Also, she finds out a lot more information and background about why something is the way it is. This helps reveal how her parents are thinking and reasoning.

Be Sensitive

Change is difficult for most human beings, especially if they have done something a certain way for many years. Elizabeth was sensitive to her parents, both in suggesting that they make changes and in the timing of their conversations. She waited until she and her parents were in a relaxed situation to ask if they needed help getting organized. She also made it a point to involve the other siblings once she discovered more about their parents' situation. This kept the parents from feeling like the kids were ganging up on them. Involving the siblings shows sensitivity to their feelings; some will want to be involved in helping with the parents, and some just want to know that they are not left out of decisions. Still others may feel that the sibling taking charge is trying to change something they are comfortable with or cheat them out of something.

Elizabeth is also keen on when to push an issue and when to leave it alone. When her father indicated that she might be trying to take over, she dropped the subject for the moment. Elizabeth is leveraging her good relationship with her mom to get her dad to cooperate when possible.

REFLECTIVE QUESTIONS

- What do you need to do to "observe the landscape" of your parents' lives?

- What questions can you ask them to indicate you are including them in decisions and not taking over?

- What changes might be uncomfortable for them? (*For example, allowing others to organize their belongings, getting rid of stuff or old documents*)

- What do you need to be sensitive to regarding your parents' and others' feelings regarding the situation?

WHO'S IN CHARGE?

Leadership is not about being in charge. Leadership is about taking care of those in your charge.

— SIMON SINEK

It's clear that Elizabeth is focused on what is best for her parents. She is willing to delay her trip home after Thanksgiving and cancel a ski trip to help her parents. She is thoughtful and considerate of her parents' viewpoint and her siblings' inclusion in the plan for helping them. She is more focused on her parents and her siblings, who are in her charge in a sense, than she is focused on being the boss.

Assigning Responsibility

It's time to dole out tasks in the Elder family. Elizabeth, George, and Trevor have a video call to discuss what they need to do. Susie is unable to join. Looking at the list Elizabeth has created, they make the following assignments based on everyone's experience, skillset, and proximity to their parents. Since Susie cannot join, they don't assign anything to her. They decide that they need to keep including her in their communications and continue trying to get her to participate.

Here's what the siblings considered as they determined who should do what.

Who Has the Skillset?

Since George is a physician and is close by, he chose taking charge of things that have to do with their health. In addition, he is in charge of helping in the event of a medical emergency. Elizabeth is an accomplished businesswoman and has the closest relationship with her parents, so she is the best choice for managing financial and legal decisions. Her business background and education as an MBA make her a good choice for the responsibility. She will also manage the siblings like a team and will not take over without getting input from others or sharing what she learns from legal counsel.

Who Is Close Enough?

Considering who is close enough has to do with physical proximity and solid relationships. George's wife Janice and Elizabeth's daughter, Ellen, are in close enough proximity to Walter and Mildred to help them around the house. Elizabeth called her daughter to see if she could help, given her schedule and mom duties, and she was glad to pitch in when she could make it work. Daniel and Greg live nearby and don't have family responsibilities since neither of them is married nor has kids. Both of them have a solid relationship with Walter, so they are glad to help him clean out and organize the garage and storage unit. They are both sensitive to the fact that their grandfather may be stubborn about holding on to some things.

Who Is Right for the Job?

The right person for the job must be dependable, able to handle the work, and willing to accept the responsibility. Elizabeth has a powerful-enough position in her company and has the financial resources to take on the role of leading the siblings. She is also willing to make some changes in her work situation if necessary. Since she is currently single, she does not have a spouse to consider. She has also managed several teams in her work life, so she knows how to handle sticky situations. She's learned through the years that engaging people in a team is key to making it function well.

Who	What	Notes
Getting Organized		
Elizabeth	• Legal documents – estate, will • Financial accounts and documents • Contact: Lawyers, bankers, investment advisors	
Daniel and Greg	• Garage/storage unit	
Janice & Elizabeth (Ellen)	• House & home maintenance • Bills/mail/email	
George	• Medications/doctors/contact information	
Decisions to Make		
Trevor	• Keeping the house or moving • Scoping out living options, including Home Health Care	
Elizabeth	• Legal structures/financial management	
George	• Health management • Emergency plan if one of them has a medical emergency	
Keeping the Peace		
All	• Sensitive to Dad's need to be in charge • Siblings work as a team • Understand Susie's situation • Get grandkids involved when possible	
Research		
Trevor	• Available living facilities	
Elizabeth	• Tax implications • Good legal counsel	
George	• Medicaid/Medicare/payment for helpers if one of them gets sick	

The Elder Story Continues

Each sibling, except for Susie, started with a list of tasks to accomplish based on their assignments. George, Elizabeth, and Trevor agreed that they needed to be careful and sensitive to the fact that their parents had not sent them on these missions and that they always needed to respect their parents' dignity and their need to be in charge.

All the siblings agreed that Elizabeth was the best person to take the lead in legal and financial matters. This meant she would need legal power of attorney to speak directly to their parents' legal and financial counsel.

Let's continue the story with what each sibling did.

Elizabeth

After the Thanksgiving blowup and over the Christmas holidays, Elizabeth makes some headway with her parents by getting them to agree to receive her help. Her dad reluctantly agrees to allow her to talk to their banker, accountant, and lawyer. Elizabeth explains to her parents that she needs a legal power of attorney to communicate directly with their financial professionals. It wasn't that her parents had done a bad job of planning over the years, but the tax laws had changed, and she wants to make sure no one takes advantage of them.

Though they had used the same bank, CPA firm, investment firm, and law firm for fifty years, their accounts and affairs were handed down to younger associates. Even though their lawyer still went to the office every day, he was not active in the practice of law anymore.

George and Elizabeth have ongoing conversations during this time to make sure they are on the same page and working together to help their parents. George discovers some things that have legal implications, which he shared with Elizabeth since she was handling legal matters.

Legal

Elizabeth collects all the copies of the wills that her parents told her about. One was the handwritten will she discovered over Christmas, but she finds another one in the freezer. They also have some other legal documents in the freezer, so she gathers them up and takes them to her meeting with their lawyer.

Walter is reluctant to give Elizabeth power of attorney, but Mildred convinces him it is the right thing to do. Elizabeth also suggests that they get a medical power of attorney (MPOA) while at the attorney's office in case something happens to one of them. Walter balks, but Mildred convinces him that Elizabeth is not trying to take over.

Then Elizabeth says, "Dad, I know we are making adjustments that are new for you. I can speak for the rest of my siblings when I say that all of us are so appreciative of what you have done for us through the years that we want to make sure you guys are okay. You have always been a strong tower for us, and we want you to enjoy life now that you are retired."

She takes her mom and dad to the first meeting with the law firm to get power of attorneys signed, which makes it possible for Elizabeth to deal with the law firm directly. The young lawyer, Jim Gardner, is glad to know that the other siblings agree with Elizabeth having legal power of attorney. The lawyer had prepared legal power of attorneys as well as medical power of attorneys with HIPAA language in the documents. He explains that this will allow Elizabeth access to medical records if she needs it.

In addition, Gardner had prepared a Directive to Physicians document and asks Walter and Mildred if they want these documents as well. He explains that this will make sure that people followed their wishes regarding life support. Walter makes a face as if to say *I'm not dead yet*, but Mildred reminds him that this will ensure that people follow his wishes.

To everyone's surprise, the law firm has yet another version of a will dated after the handwritten will and the will Walter kept in the freezer, so they review the will again later with Elizabeth present. They set up a separate appointment so Elizabeth will have time to read the will before discussing it with her parents' attorneys.

Banking and Investments

Elizabeth discovers that her parents had consolidated banking and investments with one institution, as their bank now had an investment arm.

Elizabeth and George put their names on the accounts. This way, no one could move any money without countersignatures. Walter is a bit annoyed about this, but Mildred reminds him that he gave a large sum of money to a friend without telling her. Walter rolls his eyes and doesn't say anything else.

George

With Elizabeth's help, George convinces his mom and dad to come up with a plan in case one of them has a medical emergency. His idea is to begin enrolling them into Medicare; however, they already had it in place. George is relieved to know that his parents have taken care of it themselves.

George also does a little research on in-home health care and how it could be funded. He finds out in-home health care can be funded through private-pay, long-term health-care insurance policies or through Medicaid. Private pay can be costly, depending upon the hourly rate and experience of the caregiver. In most cases, long-term health care must be purchased at an earlier age to qualify. Medicaid can cover in-home health care as well, but certain qualifications must be met and the requirements can vary from state to state.

Medicare and Medicaid

George did his homework regarding Medicare, the federal health insurance program. He discovered that Medicare covers the following:
- People who are sixty-five or older
- Certain younger people with disabilities
- People with end-stage renal disease (permanent kidney failure requiring dialysis or a transplant, sometimes called ESRD)

The different parts of Medicare help cover specific services:

Medicare Part A (Hospital Insurance)

Part A covers inpatient hospital stays, care in a skilled nursing facility, hospice care, and some home health care.

Medicare Part B (Medical Insurance)
Part B covers certain doctors' services, outpatient care, medical supplies, and preventive services.

Medicare Part D (Prescription Drug Coverage)
Part D adds prescription drug coverage to the following:
- Original Medicare
- Some Medicare Cost Plans
- Some Medicare Private-Fee-for-Service Plans
- Medicare Medical Savings Account Plans

These plans are offered by insurance companies and other private companies approved by Medicare. Medicare Advantage Plans may also offer prescription drug coverage that follows the same rules as Medicare Prescription Drug Plans.[3]

Medical Records, Medication, and Physician
George reviews the spreadsheet with the medical information Elizabeth had gathered. As a medical doctor, George is a bit concerned about his father's memory lapses. He calls his dad's doctor who was listed on a prescription to make a connection. Though he knows the doctor can't give him any information without Walter's consent, he wants to express his concerns and let the doctor know who he is. John Anderson, MD, Walter's doctor, is responsive to George and thanks him for making the connection. He is glad to know that family members are paying attention to behavioral changes in their loved ones.

Emergency Plan
George draws up an emergency plan to leave in the house in case something happens to one of his parents unexpectedly. It includes names of doctors and their contact information, all the siblings' contact information, and insurance and medication listings.

---

3   Medicare.gov

George also lists all their allergies. He knows that Elizabeth was working with the attorneys and her parents to get medical power of attorneys signed.

George asks his mom to post the emergency plan on the refrigerator, just in case of an unexpected crisis. That way a medical worker in the house trying to help them would have access to pertinent contacts and information.

Walter sees the plan and asks his wife about it but didn't like her answer. He says, "We don't need this!" as he took the paper down and threw it in a drawer.

This reaction from Walter is becoming more common. As family members continue to work with Walter and Mildred to get organized, they notice that Walter is moodier and, at times, extremely irritated. Even his grandsons Daniel and Greg, with whom he has always had a good relationship, have noticed a drastic change.

Trevor

Since Thanksgiving, Trevor has been scurrying around, trying to figure out how to refinance the business loan he had with his parents. That activity, plus keeping up with three teenagers—Ben, Luke, and Sarah—and all their activities, keeps him from doing what he promised concerning his parents' situation. Also, Trevor feels a little uneasy about looking into eldercare facilities when his parents had given no indication of wanting to do that.

Susie

Elizabeth and Trevor both call Susie to see how she can help. She just makes excuses about how busy she is and says she is looking for a job to help her husband pay their bills. Elizabeth decides not to assign her any duties because she doesn't think she will be very dependable. Also, she is glad to see that Susie is trying to contribute to her household finances since Susie had been dependent on their parents in the past.

Elizabeth doesn't know their dad recently told Susie she needed to pay Mildred and Walter back some of the money they had given her. Walter and Susie had a big blowup over that. He got angrier than she had ever seen him. Mildred just kept her distance. She didn't want to interfere with Walter asking Susie to pay the money back because it wasn't fair to the other siblings that Susie owed them money. Trevor was the only other one who ever approached them for financial help, and he had a plan in place to pay them back.

Walter and Mildred don't hear from Susie for several weeks, and they don't reach out to her either. They are waiting for her to offer some sort of payback plan that fits her budget. It is hard on Mildred to avoid reaching out, but she knows it is the best thing to do.

Walter

The siblings feel like they are getting on top of things. Mildred again admits that the house is a little too much for her. Even Walter admits that he needs to slow down. He gladly accepts the help of Daniel and Greg to clean out the garage. It seems the siblings' plan is going smoothly without being too intrusive. Things are going well enough that Elizabeth returns home to try to catch up on some work and her own life.

Then, Elizabeth gets a harrowing call from their mom.

"Honey, it's your dad. He's fallen and can't move. He can't talk either."

"Mom, call 911; I'll let George know."

"Okay," her mom says through tears, "I don't know what I'm going to do."

"Mom, call 911. They will get there quickly, and they know exactly what to do for him."

Elizabeth hangs up and calls George right away. George doesn't answer because he is performing surgery. Then she calls Trevor and Susie and promises to call back when she has more information. Now that she has informed the siblings, she calls Janice, George's wife, since she's a nurse, to let her know what is going on.

Next, she books a flight home. She calls an emergency meeting with her assistant to let her know that she will be leaving right away and be gone for at least several days. Fortunately, she and her assistant had already worked out a plan in case of an emergency.

When the emergency medical technicians (EMTs) arrive at the house, they immediately get to work on Walter. Since he is still conscious and his heart seems okay, they are not totally sure of the problem without further testing. By this time, Mildred is sobbing uncontrollably. When her neighbor, Sharon, sees the ambulance, she comes running over to see if she can help. Mildred just falls into her arms saying she doesn't know what to do. Sharon assures her that everything will turn out fine, that the EMTs know just what to do.

The emergency crew put Walter in the ambulance, and Sharon says she will drive Mildred to the hospital. As they are getting in the car to follow the ambulance, Susie shows up. She is visibly upset about her dad and asks if she can drive her mom to the hospital. Mildred says she is fine and will go with Sharon. Mildred does not want to upset Walter by having the kids around right away. She knows Walter is still upset with Susie from the blowup about the money she owed them.

Susie says nothing, gets in her car, and drives away. On the way to the hospital, Mildred starts to cry. Sharon softly says, "I know that was hard to tell Susie not to go to the hospital, but you do have to think of the best situation for Walter in his condition."

Mildred thanks Sharon for her support.

At the Hospital

The ER doctors are trying to figure out what caused Walter to collapse. They suspect a stroke, but they have to do some tests to verify that. They stabilize him and check him into the hospital.

Meanwhile, George finishes his surgery and sees the messages from Elizabeth and Janice. He immediately knows something was wrong and is concerned. When he learns what happened to his dad, he rushes to the ER to see what is going on. By that time, Walter has been moved to a private room. Janice is there with Mildred and tells Sharon she can go home. Mildred objects and asks Sharon to stay, but Janice is not pleased with this because Sharon seems to intrude on family dealings and doesn't always give Mildred very good advice. Janice decides not to say anything further for Walter's sake.

Walter's primary care doctor, John Anderson, gets to the hospital and is briefed on Walter's condition. When Dr. Anderson meets with Mildred to explain Walter's condition, George and Janice are there with her to ask additional questions and make sure she understands what is going on. Fortunately, Sharon realizes she should leave the room while the doctor is meeting with the family. Doctor Anderson explains that Walter had a mild stroke. He isn't sure how long it will be before Walter can talk or communicate with them. Dr. Anderson says they will start with some stroke rehabilitation therapies while Walter is still in the hospital. He recommends short-term, in-home health care for him.

George is thankful that Elizabeth has gotten the medical power of attorney signed in her last meeting with Walter and Mildred's attorney. He knows they had avoided complications by doing that.

After the meeting with Walter's doctor, George and Janice let Sharon know they will drive Mildred home because they have some family matters to discuss. Sharon is gracious about it and tells them to please let her know how she can help.

On the way home, Mildred starts softly crying.

Janice consoles her by saying, "I can imagine this is all scary to you. We all love Dad so much."

Mildred replies, "Well, I just don't know what to do. I have not been involved in the handling of all the finances and things. If he can't talk, I'm afraid I won't know what to do."

George assures his mom that they are all there to support her. He tells her that Elizabeth is on the way home and would be there by her side for at least the next few days.

Mildred seems relieved to know that Elizabeth is on the way home. She always had the closest relationship with her, and the most trust. Mildred says she doesn't want to be alone that night, so she let Janice stay over.

Lessons Learned

Estate Planning Documents – Financial/Medical

All the documents below need to be in place before someone is mentally incapacitated and long before a medical emergency.

- Last will and testament
- Financial durable power of attorney (POA)
- Medical power of attorney (MPOA)
- Living trusts and irrevocable trust – can serve as asset protection in many cases or help with continuity of authority
- Appointment of guardian over your estate and person—designating who you do or don't want in that role
- Choose POA based on skillset
- Directive to physicians

Task/Research Assignments

Assigning tasks to different family members will ensure that one person doesn't get stuck doing everything. Tasks and research should be assigned to someone who will carry through and has some level of knowledge in the area they are dealing with. If someone in the family is a physician, it makes sense that they would handle medical-type tasks. In addition, the person's relationship with the elder loved one impacts the tasks assigned to them. For example, financial information and responsibility should be handled by someone the elder loved ones trust; someone who will not take advantage of them.

Legal Documents in Place

A medical power of attorney grants a person you choose the power to make medical decisions for you if you become incapacitated. However, you must sign the document before you become incapacitated. An incapacitated individual cannot grant that power.

However, if you become incapacitated and do not have a medical power of attorney, a family member may still have the power to consent to medical treatment on your behalf.

For example, Texas law provides that if an adult patient in a hospital is incapacitated, an adult can act as a surrogate.

In the order of priority, the following people can consent to your treatment:

1. Your spouse

2. Your adult child, with the waiver and consent of all other qualified adult children to act as the sole decision-maker
3. Most of your children who are reasonably available
4. Your parents
5. An individual clearly identified to act on your behalf before you became incapacitated, your nearest living relative, or a member of the clergy

This appears to cover all situations that could arise so that a medical power of attorney would not be needed at all, but this is not the case. In many real-life situations, such as where parents are estranged from their children and haven't spoken to them in years, children aren't readily available and precious time can be wasted during a life-threatening situation with no one to make a decision.

Having a medical power of attorney in place is the only way to ensure that the person you choose can make medical decisions on your behalf.

Emergency Plan

The family did not expect Walter to collapse. Planning ahead meant the medical emergency workers had the pertinent information they needed to treat Walter.

If you have elder loved ones, it's a good idea to make sure they have a plan available. If they don't, you can suggest they do that for their own safety, or you can help them put the information together. As with other situations we have mentioned, it's always important to be aware of their feelings and handle communication appropriately.

REFLECTIVE QUESTIONS

- Who are the players in your family, and what would be the best roles for them in caring for your elder loved ones?

- What do you need to do behind the scenes to prepare for caring for your elder loved ones?

- What team issues might you and your siblings or interested parties run into in managing your elder loved ones' affairs?

- Do you have an emergency plan in place?

RELATIONSHIP DYNAMICS

Elizabeth gets George to call Trevor and Susie since he has actually talked to Walter's doctor and, as a physician, will be the best person to answer questions. Trevor does not express what is going on in his heart. He is very concerned about his dad but feeling a little like the older siblings are taking over. This makes him uneasy because his parents always seem to favor George and Elizabeth over Susie and him. Susie is blatantly annoyed at George, almost blaming him that their father had a stroke. She wants to know why George, as a doctor, had not picked up on the signs and done something sooner. George tries to explain why the signs of a stroke are not always obvious, which just makes her angrier. Unfortunately, the history of relationship dynamics in this family starts to come into the picture. Old garbage and jealousies start to appear, which does not make the situation any easier for anyone.

Walter and Mildred's pastor, Andrew Limon, is alerted since Walter is in the hospital. He visits Walter and prays over him, even though Walter cannot talk. Pastor Limon calls Mildred to see how he or anyone at the church can help. She is too frazzled to even answer and suggests he call Elizabeth. Mildred knows that Elizabeth will know what to tell him.

When Trevor told Ben, Luke, and Sarah about their grandfather, they are all upset. He tells Ben via phone, and Ben is worried that Grandpa might die. Trevor speaks to Luke when he gets home from basketball practice. Luke says he can't believe that his grandpa can't talk. When Sarah, who is at home doing homework, hears the news, she just bursts into tears and will not share her feelings with her dad.

Mary Stotzer, the woman from the supper club to whom Walter gave money, calls the house and leaves a message. Mildred just can't bear to talk to her. She decides to have Elizabeth call her back.

The day after Walter has the stroke, Elizabeth arrives. She takes a cab to Mildred and Walter's house and finds her mother in shambles. Mildred is grateful to see Elizabeth and secretly hopes she can just stay and handle everything. Mildred is feeling so overwhelmed that she cannot think clearly.

Elizabeth starts to feel a little overwhelmed herself and puts several large projects on hold at her company, at the risk of problems arising while she is gone. She feels the pressure of not showing her own anxiety to her mother, knowing her mother is struggling to deal with all the change and the fear that she might lose Walter.

As you can see throughout the story, relationship dynamics in managing your elders can have an impact in more ways than one. First, you see family dynamics among siblings, parents, and other family members like children, grandchildren, and in-laws. Second, elders have relationships with people who are not family members, including friends, caregivers, bankers, lawyers, and others who may influence their thinking and decisions. Finally, if you are the caregiver, even your relationships in your own household and with your friends can be impacted.

Family Dynamics

Families with several siblings or extended family typically have a "go-to" person who handles issues and is often the glue of the family. By glue, I mean when siblings have disagreements with the family as a whole or disagreements with each other, this person typically facilitates smoothing things out. When family members make foolish decisions or take advantage of their parents or elder loved ones, these people typically do the cleanup work. Others involved with the elders may be disrespectful, jealous, or hurt by this person's position in the family and the respect they get from others.

Earlier in the story, you saw the unfortunate family dynamics that started long before Walter and Mildred needed help managing everything. Clearly, Elizabeth ends up being the go-to person for several reasons. She has the strongest and most trusting relationship with her mom, and she's good about asking questions rather than forcing her agenda. When Susie got upset, Elizabeth didn't take offense or get defensive. Obviously, her success in business has given her some acute skills for leading a team, even if it's her own family.

These family members have been in contact with each other over the years. Unfortunately, they have not had many deep and meaningful conversations. Their belief systems are not totally aligned, so joint decision-making can be a challenge. For example, Susie feels like the government should help people in need, and George thinks that government help enables people not to pull their own weight. These opposing attitudes have damaged their relationship in other areas. George feels like Susie is a taker and lazy. He's disturbed about her taking advantage of their parents financially and feels like this stems from her attitude that someone should help those who are struggling.

Family members may not process information the same way. In the case of the Elder family, Trevor is not as detail-oriented and organized as George and Elizabeth. Susie has distanced herself from any information about her parents, and she feels like the other siblings are being overly controlling. George and Elizabeth are more detail-oriented and like to track information. Elizabeth is concerned about only keeping information Walter and Mildred really need. George is against getting rid of too many records because he doesn't trust Susie and Trevor, who have gotten money from their parents.

Walter Comes Home

After a several-day stay in the hospital, Walter comes home. It's apparent that someone other than Mildred or Elizabeth needs to take care of him, just as Dr. Anderson suggested. In addition to needing physical help to get around, Walter seems uncharacteristically quiet and depressed. He doesn't even attempt to communicate. Even though he miraculously has some speech abilities back, he is quite discouraged with his limitations due to the stroke. All his life, Walter has been a get-it-done type of person.

Now he must depend on others, and it's not a comfortable place for him.[4] His doctor suggests he see a geriatric psychiatrist to help him through the changes. Walter agrees and starts going to a geriatric psychiatrist every other week.

Elizabeth is still trying to manage her job remotely, and Mildred is totally dependent on Elizabeth. Elizabeth goes through the process of hiring someone to help, which takes her two weeks. She finds Julie Ahn and thinks she will be a good fit for her parents, so she hires her to come to the house five days a week. She is hoping this will relieve the pressure she feels to take care of her job and her parents. Elizabeth is starting to wear out with managing her mom during the day and catching up on work at night. She's asking herself why she must stop everything in her life to take care of her parents. Her resentment is not aimed toward her parents; rather, she's annoyed with her siblings who live closer and have fewer responsibilities, yet they don't seem ready to step in and help in any big way.

One evening Susie comes over to visit her dad. She talks with him briefly, and then leaves the room and invites Elizabeth to talk outside. Susie vents her anger because Elizabeth is considered the favorite child. Elizabeth, tired and annoyed with Susie's antics, loses her temper.

She explodes, "Really, Susie! I have raised my daughter alone and worked tirelessly to get where I am in my job. I'm trying to manage my job remotely and take care of Mom and Dad. What have you done to help? I feel like all you do is blame other people for your problems."

Susie retorts, "You just don't understand! You always made good grades and got what you wanted. Life has not been that easy for me."

"Easy! My life hasn't been easy. I just focused on what I needed to do to support my daughter and succeed in my job. I've been coming back and forth to help Mom and Dad *and* working at night! I'm done with this conversation."

Elizabeth goes back into the house and Susie leaves without saying goodbye to anyone.

---

[4] My interview with Delwin Williams, MD, Psychiatrist at John Peter Smith Hospital, Ft. Worth, Texas, July 2019.

Sibling Rivalry

Obviously, not all the children in the Elder family get along. It's clear that Susie feels ostracized or like she has been treated unfairly. In fact, there has been a rift between George and Susie for many years. She wanted to be a nurse but couldn't get into nursing school due to a learning disability. For years, she felt that George and Janice looked down their noses at her. When George found out that Walter and Mildred had helped Susie financially, that did not help the already stressed relationship.

At one point, Susie tried to get her parents to give her a beautiful Oriental rug that had been in the family for generations. Her mom didn't say anything, but it really hurt her feelings. She felt like Susie couldn't wait for them to pass away to get the rug. When the rest of the kids found out about this, they were furious—not because they wanted the rug but because Susie always seemed to want a handout. They all wondered why she didn't just get a job. It wasn't like she was unemployable.

Forgiveness

Susie and Trevor feel resentment toward their older siblings, which stems from feeling like they were not the favored ones in their family. At this point, Trevor and Susie are stumbling in the mindset of "it's not fair." Both of them, to different degrees, feel they have been slighted. George resents Susie for bilking money from their parents. He shows his negative attitude toward Susie in the way he communicates with her.

According to the Mayo Foundation for Medical Education and Research, all of them need to learn to forgive or they could get physically sick.[5]

Although it has not come out in the story, Mildred is disappointed with Trevor for not paying his loan back. She feels like this has caused strife among the siblings, which makes her sad. She has never shared her feelings about this with him, but it has been eating away at her for about five years.

---

5 Mayo Clinic Staff, "Forgiveness: Letting go of grudges and bitterness," https://www.mayoclinic.org/healthy-lifestyle/adult-health/in-depth/forgiveness/art-20047692

When she brings it up to Walter, he just says, "Well, he's doing the best he can, and he has those three kids to raise."

Mildred always thinks to herself that they raised four kids and managed their finances themselves, yet Walter makes excuses for Trevor. She feels close to Elizabeth because she never made excuses. She always worked very hard, whether it was on schoolwork, college studies, or moving up in corporate America. Elizabeth always just did what she needed to do in any situation.

Friends

Friends can be a help or a hindrance. Some may try to influence your elder loved ones and give them bad advice. Those who can be trusted to do what's best for your loved ones can help you get them to do things they need to do. In the story, Janice is concerned about Sharon the neighbor because Janice feels like she gives Mildred bad advice. Sharon has told Mildred she should be careful about trusting her kids too much because she has seen many of her friends' kids take over a situation when the parents get older. She's told Mildred that she is sure her kids love her, but they also might want some of the money that Walter worked hard to earn.

The Caregiver Arrives

It's been two weeks since Walter came home. Everyone is exhausted. Elizabeth has physically been away from work and is managing everything remotely. All the other siblings seem to be busy with other things. The brunt of supporting Walter and Mildred has fallen solely on Elizabeth.

Julie Ahn, the caregiver, arrives on a Monday morning and seems quite able to take care of Walter and Mildred. At the end of the week, Elizabeth decides it's time to go home. Mildred is not totally comfortable with that. However, as much as she wants to stay and support her mom, Elizabeth needs to get back to her job and back home to rejuvenate.

Julie comes in Monday through Friday, and Janice comes to Walter and Mildred's on the weekends. George is too busy with patients to help much, Trevor is trying to keep his business afloat, and Susie has a job now and doesn't know how she can fit her parents into her schedule.

No one is paying too much attention to how the caregiver is working out until Elizabeth happens to have a phone conversation with her mother. Mildred explains that Julie sometimes arrives two hours late. This means that Mildred, who is tiring from her own medical issues, must figure out how to take care of Walter on her own. Mildred doesn't know what to do beyond filling in the gaps where the caregiver fails.

A week later, Elizabeth gets a call from her mom because Julie didn't show up for work. Elizabeth calls the agency that placed Julie in their home to find out what is going on. It turns out that Julie had to quit because her own mother had a debilitating heart attack. The agency was supposed to send an emergency backup caregiver but failed to do so.

Elizabeth calls George and says, "George, you have to help me here. I can't keep leaving work for weeks on end to manage things with Mom and Dad. Can you guys figure out the caregiver situation since you are there? I just can't do this right now."

George agrees to help and calls the agency to get the caregiver situation straightened out. The agency sends a new caregiver who they think will work out. After about two weeks, it's apparent that this person won't work either.

Her attitude toward Walter and Mildred is condescending. This caretaker seems to lose track of Walter too. One time Walter wandered down the street and got confused about how to get home. Fortunately, a neighbor saw him and took him home. Walter was extremely embarrassed about the incident, and it further chipped away at his waning pride of being the leader of the family.

George decides it might be time for his parents to move to a safer location for Walter. He calls a family meeting with the siblings and declares that it's time to get Mom and Dad into a retirement community. Elizabeth attends the meeting virtually. Trevor, who has not done his homework on the retirement home options he was responsible for, doesn't say much. Susie thinks sending them out of their house is not a good idea and they should just find a reliable caregiver who can come to the house. George and Elizabeth, who have spent the most time taking care of their parents, strategize how to facilitate the conversation with their parents about moving to a retirement community.

Elizabeth makes a trip home to speak to them in person. When Elizabeth arrives, she takes a cab to her parents' house. Mildred is sure that Elizabeth has arrived for good and is elated that she is there. Elizabeth is feeling taxed and annoyed that the siblings who live near their parents are not pulling their load. All the stress of her job and going back and forth to her parents' home has taken its toll on her health. She has started getting migraine headaches and suffering from fatigue. These illnesses have created havoc with her job. In the last few months, her team has missed several major project deadlines due to her absence. Elizabeth is about at the end of her endurance. She is not typically a resentful person, but she finds negative thoughts toward her siblings creeping in.

Walter and Mildred are now both becoming forgetful, which doesn't help matters. Elizabeth feels her parents' situation is too big for her.

Assisted-Living Community

During and after the family meeting, the siblings consider several options. One would be to have formal and informal caregivers. In that case, they would hire a new caregiver but have Tom Spencer and Sharon check on them from time to time and be a backup for the caregiver. They also think about getting Mildred and Walter's church to help. All in all, they decide trying to keep their parents at home will require more coordination than any of them can commit to.

Finding the right place for Walter and Mildred takes a lot of research. Greg and Daniel help by going with them to some of the locations. They are not only interested in the features or amenities; they are also looking for how the staff treats the people who live there. Walter is open to the feedback that Daniel and Greg gave him, due to their solid relationships with them. This goes back to the time when they were very small boys and spent a lot of time with Walter puttering around the garage and going on weekend outings with him.

Ultimately, the Elders realize it's time to make a change and move to an assisted- living residence. They understand this means someone can cook for them, or they can eat in the centralized cafeteria. If Walter needs physical help for something like getting dressed, someone is there to help.

Someone will always check on them to make sure they take their medicine and don't get it mixed up.

Elizabeth's close relationship with her parents impacts their decision to get legal documents in order and move out of their house. The fact that Elizabeth is more focused on their well-being than her selfish interests helps them see that the retirement home is the best option for them.

Daniel helps them get their home ready to sell. At one time, Daniel was a realtor, so he has connections with people who could repair the property and determine a good price. Cleaning out Walter and Mildred's lifetime of collected stuff was a different story.

Susie asks again if she can have the Oriental rug that has been in Mildred's family for generations. Mildred does not say anything, but it really hurts her feelings. She is getting annoyed at Susie always wanting a handout.

The family decides to put several things in storage until they have time to sort through all of it. Getting their parents to a place with the medical support they need is urgent at this point, so cleaning out can wait.

After the move, Walter makes great improvements from his stroke, and Mildred is glad that someone else is doing the cooking. As Walter continues to recover, they are quick to get all their legal documents in order. They think about and appoint the right people to take care of their affairs if something happens to one or both of them, and they have their attorney prepare the documents they need.

Walter Fades

Fortunately, the Elders got their legal affairs in order before Walter's dementia got worse. It gets to the point where Mildred feels she has lost her husband, even though he is still alive. The assisted-living residence is a lifesaver because the Elders can have their meals fixed for them, someone is consistently checking on them and making sure they are taking meds, and Walter has the physical help he needs.

Mildred becomes vulnerable because she gets lonely from being unable to communicate with Walter as she had for so many years. Some scammers start calling her on the phone, and she believes whatever they tell her. One time she shares this with Elizabeth, who then gets Mildred a call-blocker app to block spam and scam calls.

Elizabeth also notices that Mildred is making lots of contributions to various organizations. Mildred would just send a little check to anyone who solicited funds. Elizabeth is concerned that organizations are taking advantage of her mom. She has to visit with her mom about what is reasonable for her parents' budget.

When she was younger, Mildred played bridge weekly. She tries joining a bridge group in the assisted-living community but soon drops out because she is worried about leaving Walter. Helpers in the facility assure her they will watch over Walter while she plays cards or that he can go sit and watch. The real issue is that Mildred is getting depressed about feeling old and lonely. She doesn't have the passion for bridge anymore and is frustrated that she can't play as well as in her younger years.

Trevor and his wife Stacy try cheering her up by suggesting she go out with them to a play, the movies, or for supper. She always declines. Nothing will bring her husband back to his right mind. Mildred just tries to be grateful for the good days with Walter when he acted more like the man she married.

All the siblings do everything that they can think of to cheer up their mom, from taking grandkids to the assisted-living residence for lunch to planning birthday celebrations for Mom and Dad. These events get their mom's mind off "losing" Walter for a little while.

Issues You May Face

Though you may not face issues with helping your elderly parents manage their lives, if you do have to help them due to their dementia or other issues with aging, there's no easy, cookie-cutter solution or set process. In addition, if several siblings or other relatives are involved, the situation can become more complicated. People are people, and, unfortunately, sometimes they are more focused on their own personal needs than the needs of others or the needs of the group of people involved.

You Won't Agree on Everything

As siblings or interested parties around elder family members, you probably will not agree on everything. Sometimes you may have to agree to disagree to keep moving forward. A key here is to keep communication lines open. If you disagree and don't share your opinion, that could fester and turn into anger or resentment that works against the goal you and your siblings have for helping your parents.

Grown Apart

You and your siblings likely haven't lived together for a while and may have differences of opinion and be coming from different places in life. All the siblings or people around elder family members have their own set of problems or challenges, which can impact working together in what can often be a stressful situation.

In the story, we see that Susie has been dependent on her parents financially for many years, which has driven her away from the other siblings. It's under the radar and no one talks about it, but it is very real in the relationship dynamics among the siblings.

Even though these siblings see each other once a year or so, Susie has distanced herself from the others. She doesn't have much of a relationship with any of them, which causes issues when Elizabeth is trying to get the siblings to help.

Can You Work as a Team?

Why even consider these issues? You need to work together as a team, keeping your parents' best interests in mind, as you would want when you get older. Anything you can do to move toward that will help all of you in the long term. You can't control other people's behavior. Someone in your group of interested parties, like Susie, may not want to engage with the rest of you. And the siblings must deal with this. At Elizabeth's direction, they have agreed to try to understand Susie's viewpoint rather than get mad about the financial assistance she has received from their parents.

Every family has its own set of issues. Sometimes they do not even surface until inheritance, control of assets, and decisions about parents arise.

Be ready for the unexpected when you are dealing with siblings, especially if you have lived away from each other for a while. Part of working with a team is dealing with the issues that arise and still effectively working toward your goal.

Even if you have been in contact with each other, you may have very different perspectives about how things should be handled. This can be based on birth order, relationships with parents growing up and through the adult years, financial or family status, and underlying belief systems. To work as a team, people may have to sometimes put aside what they want or let go of control.

Lessons Learned

This family was blessed that Walter recovered to the point that they could continue to get things in order. The relationships in the story played a key role in getting Walter and Mildred to the right situation in the assisted-living community.

Though Elizabeth carried the brunt of the load, she finally spoke up about the things eating at her. The go-to person in a family needs to speak up if they are overwhelmed. Others may not realize the person needs or wants help. This is especially true if patterns of family dynamics have been set over the years. You can see from the story that old wounds probably still exist between Susie and Elizabeth. Elizabeth finally has enough and explodes at Susie.

Leverage the solid relationships in the family to help your elder loved ones. Daniel and Greg helped Walter and Mildred decide on the right place for themselves. They could do this because of a long-standing and special relationship with Walter.

The status quo can be hard to break. For example, the longer Trevor dragged out paying the loan back, the harder it was for Walter and Mildred to strictly enforce the payment plan. Susie's distancing herself from the other siblings became something everyone expected. When it was time to assign tasks regarding their parents, everyone let her off the hook due to her history.

RELATIONSHIP DYNAMICS

REFLECTIVE QUESTIONS

- How well can you and your siblings and other family members work together in managing relationship issues?

- What issues of sibling rivalry do you face or anticipate in dealing with your parents or loved ones?

- What issues do you see with other relationship dynamics, with friends and other people close to the family?

- What is your role in facilitating better relationship dynamics?

CREATIVE CAREGIVING AND BEYOND

KEEPING YOUR SANITY AND THEIR DIGNITY

Honor your father and your mother, that your days may be long in the land that the Lord your God is giving you.

— **EXODUS 20:12 ESV**

Elizabeth worked hard to maintain her parents' dignity. Eventually, she started to tire out because she put her parents' needs before her own. In the balance of keeping her sanity and maintaining her parents' dignity, she was slowly losing the battle.

Certainly, you want to maintain your parents' dignity in the process of caring for them as they age, but this becomes more and more challenging when they have issues with dementia and failing health and can do fewer things for themselves. You must remember to take care of yourself because if you don't and your health fails, you can't help them either. You must work at maintaining your sanity too. That is just as important as maintaining their dignity. Below is a story about a woman who dedicated her life to caring for her mother to the detriment of her own health.

The Toll of Caregiving

As you can see from the Elder family story, Elizabeth's commitment to her parents' well-being took its toll on her and her health. The extra coordination with her assistant to manage her job, trips home to manage her parents' situation, and her own health issues ultimately took their toll on her, to the point that she erupted at her sister, Susie.

Elizabeth finally asked George to pull a little more weight. Her frustration with her siblings was building so much that her attitude was deteriorating.

Taking up for yourself is critical in these types of situations. You are the only one who can stand up for yourself so that people don't take advantage of you.

Maintaining Your Sanity

Keeping your sanity is important. You can't let caring for your parents rob you of caring for yourself. Take care of yourself physically and mentally so your frustration doesn't spill over and impact your communication with your loved one. Sometimes you have to let go of control. Elizabeth probably could have been more forceful in getting her siblings to take on responsibility. This might have saved her from her ultimate health issues.

Taking care of yourself is not just about you. It's also about how your parent feels. Your parent may feel frustrated because he or she cannot do what they used to. If you get annoyed with them for something they can't control, they might lash out at you or sink into depression.

Caregiver Burnout

One thing you want to avoid is caregiver burnout. If you get to that point, you are no help to anyone.

According to HelpGuide, a nonprofit mental health and wellness website, Caregiver burnout is a state of emotional, mental, and physical exhaustion caused by the prolonged and overwhelming stress of caregiving. While caring for a loved one can be very rewarding, it also involves many stressors. And since caregiving is often a long-term challenge, the stress it generates can be particularly damaging. You may face years or even decades of caregiving responsibilities. It can be disheartening when there's no hope that your family member will get better or if, despite your best efforts, their condition is gradually deteriorating.

If you don't get the physical and emotional support you need, the stress of caregiving can leave you vulnerable to a wide range of problems, including depression, anxiety, and eventually burnout. And when you get to that point, both you and the person you're caring for suffer. That's why managing the stress levels in your life is just as important as making sure your family member gets to their doctor's appointment or takes their medication on time. No matter how stressful your caregiving responsibilities or how bleak your situation seems, there are plenty of things you can do to ease your stress levels, avoid caregiver burnout, and start to feel positive and hopeful again.[6]

Below are some common signs to watch for to see if you are close to burnout and some signs you have caregiver burnout.

Common Signs and Symptoms of Caregiver Stress
- Anxiety, depression, irritability
- Feeling tired and run down
- Difficulty sleeping
- Overreacting to minor nuisances
- New or worsening health problems
- Trouble concentrating
- Feeling increasingly resentful
- Drinking, smoking, or eating more
- Neglecting responsibilities
- Cutting back on leisure activities

Common Signs and Symptoms of Caregiver Burnout
- You have much less energy than you once had
- It seems like you catch every cold or bout of flu that's going around

---

6 Melinda Smith, "Caregiver Stress and Burnout," https://www.helpguide.org/articles/stress/caregiver-stress-and-burnout.htm/

- You're constantly exhausted, even after sleeping or taking a break[7]

Avoid Caregiver Burnout

The best strategy for you as a caregiver is to avoid getting to the point of burnout in the first place. Always remember to "take the oxygen": if you ride on an airplane, you know that the flight attendant will tell you to take the oxygen first, then assist a child or someone who needs help. If you don't have any oxygen, you will pass out trying to help someone else.

As I mentioned earlier in this chapter, maintaining your sanity is just as important as protecting their dignity. If you don't, you may take out your frustration on your loved one. Your mom or dad may not be as quick mentally or physically as they once were. You, on the other hand, have taken on a whole new responsibility and set of tasks that may make you feel more harried. You must stop and breathe now and then.

- Choose empowerment
- Take care of yourself

Let's dive further into these key principles to avoid caregiver burnout.

Choose Empowerment

No matter what you do, or your situation in life, being empowered is a choice. Feeling powerless can lead to burnout and depression. As a caregiver, you can feel trapped in a role you didn't foresee. You must choose a mindset that says you aren't powerless, even when you can't obtain the extra help you want. As HelpGuide says, "You can always get more happiness and hope." Here are HelpGuide's tips, along with my advice, for choosing empowerment.

---

7   Melinda Smith, "Caregiver Stress and Burnout," https://www.helpguide.org/articles/stress/caregiver-stress-and-burnout.htm/

1. Practice acceptance

You may find yourself spending a lot of energy on the questions "Why did this happen to me?" or "Why do I have to deal with this when I have siblings who could help?" This won't help you feel better. Accept the situation for what it is. Your loved one needs your support, and you care enough for them to give it. You can't wish for more hours in the day or force your brother to help out more. Rather than stressing out over things you can't control, focus on how you choose to react to problems.

2. Embrace your caregiving choice

Acknowledge that you have made a conscious choice to support your loved one. Maybe you are providing care because your parent cared for you and made sacrifices for you while you were growing up. Maybe you want to set an example for your children. Think about how caregiving has made you stronger or brought you closer to the one you are taking care of. Motivation based on your deep feelings or relationship with your loved one can carry you through the situation.

3. Don't let caregiving take over your life

Some people can feel like their life is over because a parent is moving into their home. Realize that you can still make choices to keep caregiving from taking over. Make sure you continue to do things that have meaning and purpose for you. That could be spending time with your family, volunteering at church, working on a favorite hobby, or your career.

4. Celebrate the small victories

HelpGuide advises, "If you start to feel discouraged, remind yourself that all your efforts matter. . . . Don't underestimate the importance of making your loved one feel more safe, comfortable, and loved!"[8]

---

8   Melinda Smith, "Caregiver Stress and Burnout," https://www.helpguide.org/articles/stress/caregiver-stress-and-burnout.htm/

Take Care of Yourself

As a busy caregiver, leisure time may seem like an impossible luxury. But you owe it to yourself—as well as to the person you're caring for—to carve it into your schedule. Give yourself permission to rest and to do things that you enjoy on a daily basis. You will be a better caregiver for it.

If you're not regularly taking time off to de-stress and recharge your batteries, you'll end up accomplishing less in the long run. After a break, you should feel more energetic and focused, so you'll quickly make up for your relaxation time.

1. *Maintain your personal relationships*

Don't let your friendships get lost in the shuffle of caregiving. These relationships will help sustain you and keep you positive. If it's difficult to leave the house, invite friends over to visit with you over coffee, tea, or dinner. [Educate them on the fact that you need coverage for your loved one if you have them at home. This will help your friends include you because they realize that you need to plan ahead. Make sure you get out of the house sometimes.]

2. *Share your feelings*

Expressing what you're going through can be very cathartic. Sharing your feelings with family or friends won't make you a burden to others. In fact, most people will be flattered that you trust them enough to confide in them, and it will only strengthen your bond.

3. *Find ways to pamper yourself*

Small luxuries can go a long way toward relieving stress and boosting your spirits. [Do something that makes you feel special. What little thing will rejuvenate you?]

4. *Make yourself laugh*

Laughter is an excellent antidote to stress—and a little goes a long way. Read a funny book, watch a comedy, or call a friend who makes you laugh. And whenever you can, try to find the humor in everyday situations.

5. *Take care of your own health*
- It's easy to forget about your own health when you're busy with a loved one's care. Don't skip checkups or medical appointments. You need to be healthy in order to take good care of your family member.
- When you're stressed and tired, the last thing you feel like doing is exercising. But you'll feel better afterward. Exercise is a powerful stress reliever and mood enhancer. Aim for a minimum of 30 minutes on most days—break it into three 10-minute sessions . . . [Regular exercise] boosts your energy level and helps you fight fatigue.
- Nourish your body with fresh fruit, vegetables, lean protein, and healthy fats such as fish, nuts, and olive oil, . . . which . . . will fuel you with steady energy. [Also, make sure to stay hydrated. Dehydration can cause you to feel fatigued.] Avoid sugar and caffeine, which provide a quick pick-me-up and an even quicker crash.
- [Get enough sleep.] Most people need more sleep than they think. When you get less, your mood, energy, productivity, and ability to handle stress will suffer.[9]

Keeping Their Dignity

To keep your loved ones' dignity, you must be creative. You are protecting yourself from caregiver burnout while at the same time trying to manage your parents' dignity. It can definitely be a challenge. Since you are

---

[9] Melinda Smith, "Caregiver Stress and Burnout," https://www.helpguide.org/articles/stress/caregiver-stress-and-burnout.htm/

managing your own life and theirs too, you have at least a double portion to take care of.

Your loved ones may have difficulty with certain tasks, especially if they are proud people. As you saw in the Elder family story with Walter the patriarch, they may have difficulty admitting they need to stop doing some things. It takes delicate handling to create that balance between letting them feel they are in control and protecting them from harm.

Respecting Their Belongings

In the story, you saw that Elizabeth noticed she needed to help her mother clean out a room in the house where her mom had countless collectibles she had kept for many years.

She had to be aware that some things had sentimental value and created a source of comfort for her mom. To insist she give them away would not be the right thing to do. Her mother needed to make these decisions herself. In the same way, Walter did not want to give up business information, bank statements, and other documents because he thought he might need the information. Rather than Elizabeth telling him he needed to get rid of things because he didn't need them, she had the respect to ask if she could visit with his CPA to make sure they were not discarding something that they needed to keep.

When Susie asked for the rug that was in Mildred's family for generations, Mildred felt like her daughter did not respect her belongings. Even though she and Walter were moving to an assisted-living community, Mildred thought they could probably use it in their living space.

Life Is Unsettling

Even though Walter lived through the stroke, his increasing dementia robbed Mildred of her lifelong beloved one. This life change was unsettling for Mildred. They were married for sixty years, which is quite a long time to share life with someone. Sometimes people feel cut adrift when they lose a loved one who has been a part of their life for so many years. In Mildred and Walter's case, even though he was still alive, mentally he was gone.

Even though Walter recovered from his stroke, losing his freedom of being totally independent was a big change. Walter was venturing into new territory where he had never gone before. Walter was accustomed to being in charge, so moving to assisted living could be a challenge for him.

Positive Encouragement

The kids encourage their parents to leave the big house behind, but it's such a place of comfort and security for them, it's hard to imagine letting go of it. Elizabeth encourages them by focusing on the positives of moving to a place with beautiful surroundings, great food, and opportunities for social engagement.

The children focus on listening to their parents' concerns about going to an "old-folks' home." They help their parents understand that going to the assisted-living residence is a move up from trying to take care of a house that needs repair and is a lot to manage.

Protecting Them from Harm

Part of your job in respecting their dignity is protecting them from harm. Sometimes this can be a challenge because your loved ones may not want to admit that anything is wrong, or they may not even be aware of it. You may run into behavioral challenges where you must work hard to keep your cool. You may also have to deal with your own denial about the situation with your loved one.

People dealing with dementia can get creative. If you find that your loved ones should not be driving anymore, you should, of course, take the car keys away, but they may find other ways to "escape." I've known of elderly parents who called taxis; walked somewhere to purchase a bicycle; or figured out how to start the car without the keys so that their caregivers had to disconnect the battery.

In Walter's case, if he had not had a stroke, he might have tried to drive somewhere. He did manage to escape by trying to take a walk, but fortunately, a neighbor saw him and took him home. This was one of the key reasons the children wanted their parents to go to an assisted-living community. It was a way of protecting Walter from harm.

What Does This Mean for Your Sanity and Their Dignity?

As you can see, many people dealing with elders may endure unpleasant episodes and behaviors. You may feel that denying the existence of a problem is the easier route, but that won't make the problem go away. Denying the signs of dementia or mental problems will not help the situation. You cannot diagnose whether this is dementia or pseudodementia, a condition where diseases can manifest as dementia but are not a true dementia process; instead, some other physical ailment is causing symptoms that mimic dementia. The real issue can be something as simple as the sodium level being too low or a urinary tract infection.[10]

For the sake of your sanity, pay attention to your loved ones and plan for the long term. What you are noticing today probably won't go away tomorrow.

Then think about their dignity. If they get violent with you and they have not been that way before, how might that feel? Maybe they say things to you and then wonder why your feelings are hurt. Understand that your loved ones are not acting like the people you grew up with. This can be as hard on them as it is on you. Even if they resist your help, if you protect and support their dignity, you will end up with a better long-term solution.

One reason I suggest thinking ahead is that it's easier to nudge your loved ones into a different situation than to shove them there.

What's Next

A significant key to keeping your sanity and their dignity is to get help. As you can see, based on what we have discussed in this chapter, seeking competent help is not just a good idea—it's prudent. If you are a caregiver for a loved one, you are not helping anyone if you overdo it and try to take on too much. You might end up losing your sanity and sacrificing your elder's dignity.

In the next chapter, we will review key points for choosing and monitoring helpers. We'll also discuss an overall plan for keeping

---

10   My interview with Dr. Delwin Williams, MD, Psychiatrist at John Peter Smith Hospital, Ft. Worth, Texas, July 2019.

helpers in place, as sometimes life happens to them as well, so you need backup plans.

REFLECTIVE QUESTIONS

- How is your loved one processing information? Do they need help beyond what you can provide?
- How are you reacting to your elder loved one? Are you frustrated or angry, feeling exhausted or overworked? What do you need to change?
- What areas of your sanity and dignity do you need to address?

HELP TO THE RESCUE!

You do not have to do all this alone. Even if you are the go-to person in your family, remember to ask for help. It may not be easy if you are a take-charge person, but it's essential that you don't try to do it all yourself. How much help you need will depend on your situation and the conditions and abilities of one or both of your elderly parents.

Be Willing to Ask for Help

One of the first steps to finding help in caring for your loved one(s) is being willing to ask for help. You may have to change your mind-set about doing it all alone. This could come from the feeling of loyalty to your parent, who raised you and always took care of you throughout your life. You may have had other experiences or noticed situations in other families when elderly parents were neglected. You must put all these feelings and thoughts aside to make sure you do the best thing for you and your loved one.

As previously discussed, if you don't take care of yourself and you suffer from burnout, you are no help to your loved one. Getting help is a way to avoid caregiver burnout.

You might have to be vulnerable and tell people what you are feeling when managing an elderly member of the family. It might feel risky if you are not sure how people will react. Remember that you don't have control over how they react, but if you don't ask anyone for help or share where you are, you won't get help. While you can hire helpers, that can get costly, especially if you are trying to manage your own life and your family and trying to take care of a family member.

As you saw in the last chapter, you need to guard your health and your sanity to be effective. In this chapter, we will explore how to plan for incorporating helpers, including the safeguards for choosing quality people and keeping them, and backup plans. If you get too tired and worn out, you might make poor decisions or even get physically sick.

Actively Ask

People who have not taken on the responsibility of caring for their elderly parents or relatives don't know what you need or that you need help. You need to be proactive about asking people for what you need. It could be help running errands, rounding up friends to cook some meals, or just visiting your loved one in an eldercare facility or in your home so you can take a break.

Perhaps you have a circle of friends, people you know from church, or neighbors you can call on for help. They can do anything from reading to your elder loved one, to just sitting with them to keep them company and listen to their stories. In some cases, it makes sense to have someone check in on *you* on a regular basis, so you can get them to help you with what you need in the moment. It takes a little of the burden off you since you are not always calling other people for help. You'll find that many people want to help and assigning them the check-in task, even if it's only for you to get things off your mind, makes them feel good too.

Don't be shy about accepting help. When people reach out to you to offer help, it's often because they feel good when they help out. It's also okay to let them do things for you. You may have to be the one to pick up prescriptions or go with your elder loved one to the doctor, but your friend can pick up your clothes from the cleaners or do other tasks.

You can also find paid resources for some of these tasks. Several apps are available to help you find anything from dog walkers to weed pullers. You can find resources from these apps to do small maintenance tasks around the house too.

Can Your Employer Help?

Though your employer may not advertise assistance they can give, it never hurts to ask. They may not even realize how taxing caring for an elderly person can be and the potential financial burden or toll it can take on someone's time and health.

One in five US workers reports they are currently providing assistance for older relatives and friends, according to a report by the AARP Public Policy Institute. Nearly 70 percent of those who do say they had to take time off or make other work adjustments because of caregiving.[11]

Here's an example of a large corporation helping its partners with eldercare.

"In response to those kinds of needs [helping family members with taking care of children or adults] and partner feedback, Starbucks is announcing a new benefit," said Ron Crawford, vice president of benefits at Starbucks.

Starbucks has joined with Care.com to offer Care@Work, an online service connecting families and caregivers. All Starbucks partners who work at U.S. company-owned stores will receive 10 subsidized backup care days a year for kids and adults. With more than 180,000 U.S. partners, Starbucks is among the largest retailers to offer this benefit.

"This is giving our partners resources for things that happen in regular life. We wanted to give them something to help fill in the gaps," said Crawford.[12]

Even if your company doesn't offer assistance, if you ask about it, you could be a catalyst to raise awareness of the need. Taking care of elder loved ones is a growing need with the aging population.

---

11   Lynn Feinberg and Rita Choula, "Understanding the Impact of Family Caregiving on Work," https://www.aarp.org/content/dam/aarp/research/public_policy_institute/ltc/2012/understanding-impact-family-caregiving-work-AARP-ppi-ltc.pdf

12   Linda Dahlstrom, "New Starbucks benefit offers backup child and adult care," https://stories.starbucks.com/stories/2018/new-starbucks-benefit-offers-backup-child-and-adult-care/

Engage Others in the Responsibilities

Try to get as many family members involved as possible. When they are engaged in taking care of their elder loved one, they will feel part of a team. As a contributing team member, you might not have to persuade others to pitch in since you are already helping with your loved one.

A relative who lives far away can help too. Find tasks they can help with remotely. As you saw in the story, responsibilities were given to family members with the right skill set and willingness and ability to help.

You can also engage neighbors, church members, and family friends to help. Honestly, your parent may get tired of you and might like having a new face around.

Vetting, Selecting, and Managing Caregivers

Finding caregivers you know you can trust can be a challenge. Whether you are putting your parent in a facility outside the home or have home health-care specialists come into your home, you cannot be too careful. Rather than simply interviewing people in facilities or home health-care professionals, pay attention to the details. Even though an agency should be vetting anyone they send to your home, you cannot always trust that. Also, you need to make sure the person taking care of your family member is a good personality fit. You cannot be too careful when vetting caregivers because your loved one may not remember or be able to explain how they are mistreated when you are away. Here are some things to watch for:

- What is their relationship with their own family?
- What is their attitude toward elderly people? Are they respectful or impatient? How do they speak to your family member?
- What do you notice about potential in-home caregivers or employees of eldercare facilities? Do they show genuine empathy and compassion? How do the elders in the facility seem to like it?
- Ask potential caregivers situational questions. For example, "If "x" happened, how would you deal with that?" This demonstrates their decision-making ability, especially if there is an emergency.
- You can research records on eldercare facilities—most states have reviews.

Once you have hired a caretaker or placed your family member in a facility, you still need to be a watchdog. You cannot assume everything is fine but must keep a vigilant eye on caregivers to make sure they are taking good care of your loved one. You are trusting your precious family member with someone else, so after you have hired people, you need to pay attention to what they are doing and how they are interacting with your loved one.

In some cases, your loved one may need to sell their family home. You can find certified seniors real estate agents to help them downsize if they need to. Also, you can find estate sales professionals who can help them sell what they don't need so they can move to a more manageable space.

Technology Can Help!

If your loved one is uncomfortable with technology, you might have to work with them to help them become more comfortable. I have taught my mom to play her favorite songs from a playlist using voice commands when available. She feels more confident about using technology, and it has given her a little boost. What other technologies can help? If your loved one will be safe using them, these devices can give them a sense of freedom so they don't feel trapped and you feel a sense of relief.

Truly, where technology is concerned, you need to be vigilant for your loved one because they may not have the mental capacity to determine if someone is taking advantage of them. In another case, they might need to be careful in dealing with someone.

You may find that if your loved one has not grown up with technology, they may not trust it, but they could be naive about it as well. Just be vigilant about helping them with technology while at the same time protecting them from predators.

Integration

As you might imagine, smoothly coordinating and integrating family members, friends, health-care professionals, and caregivers takes some attention. You need to develop a plan that keeps everyone "in the loop." The plan should include communication and accountability guidelines or agreements, especially if you have a family member living in your home. The plan should specify who is in charge of what and outline schedule transitions.

For example, you might need to leave for work at 8:00 a.m., so your home health professional needs to be there at 7:30 a.m. to ensure a smooth transition. Or if a family member stays with your loved one during the day, he or she needs to be at your home in plenty of time to make a smooth transition. The home health professional needs to know exactly what to do and who to call, beyond 911, in case of an emergency.

If you have in-home health care, make sure to have a plan B. Your health-care provider has a life too, and something could disrupt their ability to care for your family member.

To avoid confusion, your parent's physicians and their staff need to be aware of who may be contacting them regarding their patient's health in an emergency. The better your plan, the more likely you can avoid disaster.

Beyond all the logistics of providing for your family member's comfort and safety, appropriate legal and financial documentation and management will ensure that their estate is handled properly and effectively. In the next chapter, we'll discuss legal and financial documentation and safeguards.

REFLECTIVE QUESTIONS

- Are you willing to ask for help?

- What type of help will you need? For example, maintaining your loved one's home, running errands, or someone sitting with your loved one to provide companionship?

- What resources do you have available? For example, friends, neighbors, church, or civic group.

ESTATE PLANNING ESSENTIALS

You must identify and create the proper estate planning documents to accomplish your goals and protect your loved ones. You need to insulate a loved one's assets from a major health-care crisis and lawsuits. To feel secure, you must find legal advisors who can help you fully understand how to successfully manage your assets and secure your peace of mind.

Planning your own retirement and life in your golden years will help those who care for you when you need help. How you manage your finances as you prepare for retirement will greatly impact how well it goes when others need to help you. Here are some key financial tips for retirement or pre-retirement.

Protecting Yourself

Budget Carefully
During retirement, income tends to be lower than it was in the prime earning years, and that means older adults need to look for ways to limit expenses.

Don't Be Too Generous
When grown children are struggling with their own financial lives, it can be tempting to open your bank account to them. The problem with this approach is that it can stress your finances and lead to family tension.

Plan with Your Partner

Even if you've been married to your spouse for years, it's possible that you have different visions of how to spend your retirement years.

Make Sure Your Bank Is on Your Side

Some banks cater to older clients more than others, with perks such as using larger print in communication, meeting outside of the bank, and speaking clearly without being condescending. Asking about your bank's age-friendly policies before you need them can help ensure you don't get frustrated with its policies later.

Put Fraud Safeguards in Place

As an older adult, you could be at a greater risk for financial fraud, but there are ways to reduce that risk. Family members can be alerted to large withdrawals from accounts, debit cards can be programmed to only work in certain locations, and names and numbers can be placed on "do not call" lists.

Prepare for Cognitive Decline

When it comes to managing money, signs of cognitive decline tend to show up in your sixties and seventies. It can become harder to manage bills, calculate tips, and make change. Sometimes adult children or others can help prevent bigger problems, like falling behind on bills, by noticing those red flags and stepping in to help.

Protect Your Digital Assets

If you're active on social media or have an extensive digital library of music or books, consider how to pass on those digital assets when you die. You can include your wishes in your will, pick someone to share account information with, and restrict your privacy settings now, so you're not oversharing personal details with strangers.

Get Money Help from Your Adult Children

Adult children can often play a useful role in helping you manage money as you age. It's important to enlist the support of children before experiencing a crisis or cognitive decline, so they know the basics of where to find account information if they need to. Talking through plans and wishes, and even writing out an overview of how you want to manage money as you age, can also help.

Estate Planning Documents

As much as you may not want to think about it, you may need someone else to manage your financial and legal affairs at some point. Planning ahead with these documents can save a lot of headaches for those around you if something unexpected happens to you. The following outlines some of the legal and financial documents you should put in place.

Estate Planning Documents	Description and Function
Financial Power of Attorney	A financial power of attorney is a document that gives someone else the legal power to handle financial transactions for you. That person is called the *attorney-in-fact* or *agent*. The person who signs a power of attorney making someone else their agent is called the *principal*. A power of attorney can be for a special, general, or limited purpose.
Medical Power of Attorney	A medical power of attorney gives your agent the right to make health-care decisions for you, typically when you are incapacitated.

Estate Planning Documents	Description and Function
Directive to Physicians	A directive to physicians lets your doctor and loved ones know whether you choose to remain on artificial life support if your condition is terminal or irreversible. It communicates your wishes and provides peace of mind about your end-of-life treatment options.
HIPAA (Health Insurance Portability and Accountability Act)	HIPAA Stands for the Health Insurance Portability and Accountability Act, a law designed to provide privacy standards to protect patients' medical records and other health information provided to health plans, doctors, hospitals, and other health-care providers. A HIPAA document may be used to authorize the disclosure of medical information to certain persons.
Declaration of Guardianship	A declaration of guardianship allows you to designate, by written declaration or will, who you would want to be the guardian of your person and guardian of your estate if a court found you were legally incapacitated and need a guardianship.

Estate Planning Documents	Description and Function
Will	A last will and testament is a legal document that allows you to identify your beneficiaries; designate the way your property will be distributed; nominate a legal guardian for any minor children; and nominate an executor to manage your estate, pay your debts, expenses, and taxes; and distribute your estate according to your wishes.
Trust	A trust is a legal contract in which money or assets are positioned for the benefit of another, the trustee. You can create a trust in which to hold the title to your home, cars, and accounts, specifically designating who has interests and rights to the property held in the trust. The primary reason most people create a trust is to eliminate and avoid probate court and estate taxes.

Who Makes Critical Decisions?

Two key issues you must decide for your aging parents or loved ones revolve around who should make critical decisions if they become mentally incompetent and need (1) medical planning, and (2) asset protection. These decisions must be made when your elders have a sound mind and are clear on what is going on. That's why it's so important to pay attention to small signs that indicate dementia is in progress.

As your loved one's medical needs increase due to physical or mental incapacity, you need to make sure that the right legal and medical safeguards are in place. One option is to legally preserve assets and get the required health coverage to meet your loved one's needs by qualifying for Medicaid in the event you have a nursing home crisis.

REFLECTIVE QUESTIONS

- What proactive retirement plans have you made for yourself?

- If you are taking care of an elder loved one, what retirement and long-term plans have they made for their health and finances?

- What can you do to plan for your own retirement or to help elder loved ones who need to plan for retirement and long-term care?

- What resources do you need so you can plan for retirement? Legal, financial, or insurance counsel?

YOU CAN DO THIS!

Where are you in your journey of taking care of an elder loved one? You may just be starting out and unsure of your loved one's condition. Perhaps you know your loved one's situation and you feel like you are "in over your head." Wherever you are, I sincerely hope that this book helps you along in your journey.

From my personal perspective, I know you can make it all work. My mom lives with us. I have a son and a husband, a law practice, and a full life with community service and volunteer work, and we make it work.

It is so important to be an advocate for your loved one. I spent over twelve around-the-clock days in the hospital with my mother, including spending the nights there. Even though hardworking health-care providers were tending to her, it was vitally important for me to understand and ask questions about every treatment and medication they were administering. During this process, there were a few medications that should not have been administered because my mother had been taken off them, as well as other medications that were supposed to stop yet did not stop until two days later.

If I had not been at the hospital with her asking questions as the new shift arrived, the medication causing much of the problem would have continued to be administered. Even though the doctor's notes reflected the changes to the medication, somehow the message did not get to the people administering them. As you can see, it's very important to advocate for your loved one. You are the voice that often can make the difference in their care, so they come out in a better state than when they went in. My brother is a doctor, so I've had the favor of someone to bounce things off of. Even if you don't have a doctor in the family to check things with, don't let the medical degree of your loved one's doctor intimidate you. Continue to advocate and ask questions.

As I'm writing this, I am transitioning my mother from the hospital to a skilled nursing facility rehabilitation. Based on my experience at the hospital with her, I definitely will have my own caregivers sit with my mother during her stay at the skilled nursing facility.

I don't have a large family, so I've employed some wonderful caregivers who love my mother as if she is their own. I've been very blessed. Even if you can't afford around-the-clock caregivers, maybe you can assemble a team of friends and family members who can check in and make sure your loved one is comfortable and transitioning properly. The facility is doing a great job, but they can't be all things to all people. I'm just following my heart, doing what I think is best. The facility does check in on residents every two hours, and the caregivers are just a good assurance for me that if Mom needs something, especially as she transitions and gains strength, they are there for immediate assistance.

Captain's Log, Day One – Rehab Facility

One of my caregivers brought a journal to the rehab facility so as the caregivers change shifts, they can note what happened during their shift. That keeps me updated as well so I know what to address with the staff for my mom's care plan. They are so awesome—I did not even think of having a journal. They've done this on their own, and they're logging in their thoughts and notes.

Captain's Log, Day Two – Rehab Facility

Mom's caregivers discovered the dining room and said they will take her there to eat. If it had been up to me, she still would have been eating meals in the room . . . I'm a private person and don't necessarily want to socialize with anybody else, but they said, "Hey, let's go for it and get out among the people! Get her up and moving as soon as possible." This is a great example of how loved ones can be too close to a situation and caregivers or others can give a helpful perspective.

My caregivers are sending me photos and videos of Mom working out in therapy, which is perfectly fine as long as you're not videotaping or capturing anyone else in it. It is so encouraging, and I'm sharing it with my brother, who happens to be across the world in Australia right now. It's a great way for family members to stay connected, communicate, and be encouraged.

I also created a four-way text conversation with each caregiver so we can all communicate, and each morning I send out a message. I call them TEAM JESUS! I give them a Bible verse to stand on and to speak with my mom during the day, and I just tell them how much I appreciate them.

Best regards,
Wendy Whiteman

NOTES

NOTES

NOTES

NOTES

NOTES

www.ingramcontent.com/pod-product-compliance
Lightning Source LLC
Chambersburg PA
CBHW060408130526
44592CB00046B/780